PRAISE FOR JAMES WOODF...

C000171769

'A graphic and compelling accou...
bizarre yet least-known structu...
such a good reporter is his ceas...
is the result. Superb, detailed, insightful and intensely
human, it deals with events remote from most of our lives
yet manages to tell us about ourselves and our complex
relationship with a still mysterious, ancient land.'
Sydney Morning Herald

'This is Woodford's most personal work...laced with
quietly articulated longings...That is why it is so
unexpectedly nourishing.'
Canberra Times

'An affecting piece of narrative...Woodford's cast of
characters and his raw material vary with the bewildering
richness of the Australian landscape and the fence line
on the author's city eyes is sufficiently intense to make
the book very much his own.'
Australian

'There are fascinating encounters with legendary characters of
the outback, glimpses of the remoteness and pioneering spirit
that are reality for many Australians in this millennium, and
scenes of rugged beauty in the harshest of landscapes.
A captivating tale of an Australia little known but vividly
brought to life by an accomplished author.'
Melbourne Weekly

OTHER BOOKS BY THE AUTHOR

The Wollemi Pine

The Secret Life of Wombats

THE
DOG
FENCE

A JOURNEY ACROSS THE HEART OF AUSTRALIA

JAMES WOODFORD

TEXT PUBLISHING
MELBOURNE AUSTRALIA

The Text Publishing Company
171 La Trobe Street
Melbourne Victoria 3000
Australia
www.textpublishing.com.au

Copyright © 2003 James Woodford

All rights reserved. Without limiting the rights under copyright above, no part
of this publication shall be reproduced, stored in or introduced into a retrieval
system, or transmitted in any form or by any means (electronic, mechanical,
photocopying, recording or otherwise), without the prior permission of both
the copyright owner and the publisher of this book.

Printed and bound by Griffin Press
Typeset in Centaur by J & M Typesetting
Designed by Chong Weng-ho
Maps by Tony Fankhauser

All photographs by James Woodford except for p. 106, reproduced with kind
permission of Donald Byrnes, and p. 153 with kind permission of Alec Wilson.

First published 2003, reprinted 2003
This edition published 2004

National Library of Australia
Cataloguing-in-Publication data:

Woodford, James, 1968- .
The dog fence.
ISBN 1 920885 26 9

1. Feral dogs - Control - Australia. 2. Dingo - Control -
Australia. 3. Fences - Australia. I. Title.
632.697720994

This project has been assisted by the Commonwealth Government through
the Australia Council, its arts funding and advisory body.

Australia Council
for the Arts

For Prue Woodford, her mother's daughter

A DANGEROUS TRACK

Permission is required to travel along the 5400-kilometre track which flanks the Dog Fence. Australia's most remote road is not maintained for tourists and has numerous hazards for the inexperienced adventurer. It is so isolated that stops for fuel and water may be up to 1000 kilometres apart. Emergency assistance is impossible without adequate communication equipment, and pastoralists actively discourage visitors for fear of legal liability for any injuries, or fatalities, which may occur.

CONTENTS

MAP   viii–ix

1   CIVILISATION'S BOUNDARY   1

2   THE WOMBAT FENCE   11

3   WYNBRING   36

4   DEATH FENCE   64

5   THE MOON PLAIN   80

6   ROCKETS IN LAMB LAND   96

7   THE CAT-PROOF FENCE   118

8   LAKE FROME   133

9   THE FAMOUS FENCE   157

10   FLEGGY GOES BUSH   175

11   NOTHING IS AN EXAGGERATION   192

12   DEVIL'S GATES   204

13   PICCANINNY DAWN   225

EPILOGUE   245

ACKNOWLEDGMENTS   250

BIBLIOGRAPHY   252

INDEX   257

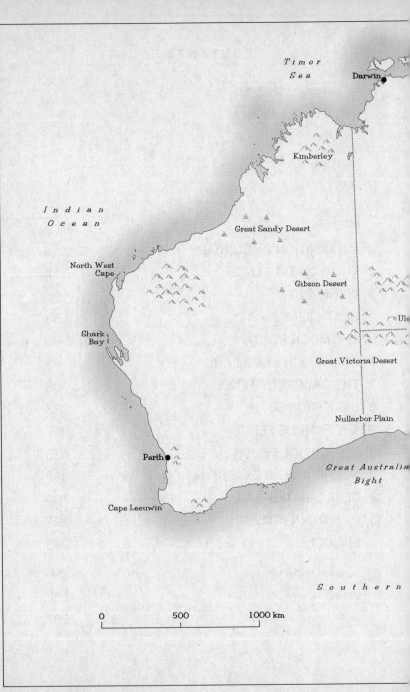

We climb onward, towards the sky and with every step my spirits rise. As I walk along, my stave striking the ground, I leave the tragic sense of things behind; I begin to smile, infused with a sense of my own foolishness, with an acceptance of the failures of this journey as well as of its wonders, acceptance of all that I might meet upon my path.

Peter Matthiessen, *The Snow Leopard*

CHAPTER 1

CIVILISATION'S BOUNDARY

Where it begins, at the Great Australian Bight just west of Penong, the Dog Fence hangs out over the Southern Ocean, topped by a single pole that points down at a seaweed-covered rockshelf. The fence ends 5400 kilometres away in Queensland, but here in South Australia a tangled strand of wire holds a five-metre length of plastic mesh in place. Immense waves roll in from the south-west and the air is humid with salt spray.

The coast is a dramatic scar, left after Gondwana finally tore itself apart. Forty million years later the sea is still surging into the gap as Antarctica and Australia continue to drift apart. The ground has numerous holes and cracks, which puff and steam like a whale's blowhole. Creep close to one of these enormous wormholes through the cliff and twenty metres below you can see a circle of the ocean, shining like a little silver eye.

It was February 2002 and I was about to begin a journey along the entire length of this extraordinary structure, designed to keep Australia's wild dog, the dingo, out of the continent's south-east corner where the richest grazing and pasture land is found.

I first crossed the fence in 1993 when I was in the Strzelecki Desert in New South Wales but, because of the sand dunes, I saw no more than a few kilometres of the structure. That day was the first I thought about travelling its length. My resolve hardened in 1995 when, while doing a story for the *Sydney Morning Herald*, I was falsely accused of spreading the rabbit calicivirus from its quarantine area in South Australia. At the time the leader of the National Party of Australia and future deputy prime minister, Tim Fischer, gave a press conference where he said, 'If proven, the reporter and photographer should be put to work on the Dog Fence between South Australia and New South Wales.' The threat only fuelled my fascination.

Whenever I was west of the Great Dividing Range, looking at almost any barrier or even when daydreaming at my desk, I often thought of the wire wall. As far as I knew it was only 600 kilometres long. One slow day in spring 2001 I pulled out an Australian atlas and started turning the pages, following the structure with my finger from one map to the next until it tipped into the Southern Ocean.

From my starting point on the New South Wales border I then tried to do the same in the opposite direction, but as soon as the line on the map entered Queensland the Dog Fence disappeared. Where did it go? How was it that I had

A dingo would have to be able to abseil to cross the Dog Fence at its starting point where it hangs over the Southern Ocean.

never known that the fence was so long?

Within an hour I had telephoned the New South Wales fence inspector, and by the end of the day I had written to the South Australian government and left a message for the Queensland boss. I had begun to plan my journey and intended on using the fence as a handrail through the heart of Australia. What sort of people would I meet? Would I be able to meet the challenges of the trip?

The desert runs hard up against the edge of the precipice and there is not a tree anywhere in sight, only saltbush, pigface, tough little grasses, rocks, boulders, pebbles and sand. Limestone coats this entire landscape like stucco for thousands of kilometres, and the ocean and the elements have carved the cliff-line into a craggy rampart. To the east are the Ocock Sandhills, which run along the coast for seven kilometres and stretch 1.5 kilometres inland. At heights of 100 metres the dunes are five times taller than the cliff where the Dog Fence starts. Beyond the cliffs, on the horizon, there seems to be an enormous ski field which is in fact more vast dunes, backing on to the fifteen-kilometre-long Dog Fence Beach. Only one spot looked safe for a dip—a tiny bay west of the fence appeared to be the perfect place to roll out a towel and take to the water.

Even on a glorious, calm day—as it was this February morning—the sound of the ocean was deafening. It is said that when a storm is battering this coastline, a noise like thunder can be heard for more than ten kilometres inland. No wonder the Great Australian Bight and the Nullarbor so terrified seamen and explorers yet simultaneously inspired respect. In the first overland crossing by a European, Edward John Eyre wrote in his diary on 10 March 1841: 'Distressing and fatal as the continuance of these cliffs might prove to us, there was a grandeur and sublimity in their appearance that was most imposing, and which struck me with admiration.'

In my bag I had an exquisite recording of Matthew Flinders' favourite woodwind music by Ignaz Pleyel. Only a few weeks earlier I had seen Flinders' flute under a glass case in Sydney. It passed by these very cliffs in January 1802 when the man who gave Australia its name was circumnavigating the great southern land. I had imagined that, on a still day, it may have been possible for Aborigines on the cliffs above the *Investigator* to have heard music drifting on the wind. Standing there, however, and struggling to even hear my companion Bill Sandow a few metres away, I knew that Flinders' music would have been taken by an eddy of wind and consumed in an instant. As I stared out to sea the continent and thousands of kilometres of fence were at my back.

Australia boasts three famous fences. In her book *Follow the Rabbit Proof Fence*, Doris Pilkington brought the Western Australian fence to public attention. Queensland, too, has its own Rabbit Proof Fence. The Dog Fence is, however, one of the longest man-made structures on Earth. Millions of trees were chopped down and turned into posts to help create it. These were then buried into the desert and slung with wire to produce an unbroken line that stretches across the continent, its sole goal to keep the dingo away from sheep. Its existence is almost an accident, a marvel of steel and wood, created in spite of quarrels between the states through which it runs.

The fence's parents are parochialism and fear, and its favourite fare is cheap labour.

The fence was built during two world wars, the Depression and several severe droughts. No single person had a vision of its existence. Rather, a series of pastoral barons and government officials have, during the last 150 years, ended up erecting pieces of a structure more in the fashion of a join-the-dots puzzle. And no one, except a handful of conservationists and scientists, ever talks seriously about pulling it down—to do so would be political suicide. Without it the sheep industry would be crippled.

The maintenance of the fence is, nevertheless, relentless work. Emus, kangaroos, wombats, echidnas, dust, sand, flood, trees, bushfires and, most of all, gravity conspire to pull it down. On maps of the continent, the fence resembles a jagged graph bisecting South Australia, New South Wales and ending in south-eastern Queensland near the coast. It is an ecological Berlin Wall comparable to the Great Wall of China, and yet most Australians have no idea what it does, whether it works, or even that it is there.

The Dog Fence, also often referred to as the Wild Dog Fence, winds its way through nuclear test sites, uranium mines, the routes of great and disastrous expeditions of exploration, through five deserts, past three giant salt lakes and it skirts regions where cultural myths like Waltzing Matilda and the Diamantina Drover were born.

Today's Dog Fence is one continuous barrier but there were once thousands of vermin fences which divided up Australia. It is estimated that in 1930, in South Australia alone, 75,000 kilometres of pest-proof wire protected farmers not only from dogs but also from rabbits and emus. The main reason for this frenzy of division was fear of dingoes. In the fourteen-year period prior to 1935, bounties were paid on 500,000 dingo scalps in South Australia. Back then there were 'dog-proof cells' established around individual farms or groups of co-operating properties that were kept dingo-free. Vermin-fenced districts were declared throughout the early twentieth century but by the end of World War II the system in South Australia was falling into disrepair. Two wealthy and influential landowners, Byron MacLachlan and Ian McTaggart, began examining the outer, northern boundaries of these vermin-fenced districts. They realised that a nearly continuous line of fence already existed from the Great Australian Bight to the New South Wales border. Rather than maintain fences inside this line, they lobbied that it would be better to concentrate on keeping *one* outer fence to protect the sheep farming regions of South Australia. On 17 June 1947 the state's Dog Fence Act came into operation and a single barrier was born, rendering tens of thousands of kilometres of old vermin fence redundant.

Archaeologist and anthropologist Scott Cane believes the Dog Fence represents much more than an obstacle to dingoes:

One crosses the Nullarbor, passes the Great Victoria Desert, goes around Coober Pedy, down to Woomera, past Marree, through Cameron Corner—where South Australia meets New South Wales and into sunny Queensland. The fence…is a great unseen and un-recognised symbol of the Australian psyche and landscape—separating the wild from the tamed—desert from pastoral and, in its remoter parts, the first from the third world of Australia.

Many Australians are aware that Aborigines have tracks and trading routes crisscrossing the entire continent, but nothing else the Europeans have built slices across Australia's landscape and history in quite the same way. The Dog Fence is the closest thing that the recent arrivals have to a songline.

But what of the animal for which the Dog Fence was built? Dingoes tend to get terrible press—most famously for the killing of Azaria Chamberlain at Uluru in 1980. Even as I planned my journey in 2001, a dingo killed an eight-year-old boy on Fraser Island.

Australia's pre-eminent dingo scientist Laurie Corbett writes that the dingo evolved from the wolf between 6000 and 10,000 years ago and became widespread throughout southern Asia:

Asian seafarers subsequently introduced dingoes into Indonesia, Borneo, the Philippines, New Guinea,

Madagascar and other islands including Australia some 3500–4000 years ago. Dingoes eventually colonised all the Australian mainland, probably assisted by the Aborigines…Some Aboriginal tribes used dingoes to hunt game, especially kangaroos, wallabies and possums. Dingoes contributed to the demise of the thylacine and other native fauna.

In recent years more scientists have begun to argue that dingoes should be protected. They believe that the dogs are not only valuable in themselves but as predators of feral pests like goats and pigs, and that we should not be restricting their territories.

Like the wolves of the northern hemisphere, dingoes hunt in packs and have complex social lives, making them a challenging enemy for graziers. By working together dogs can bring down prey far larger than themselves, such as red kangaroos and even cattle. More and more people today keep dingoes as pets but they are not an animal suited to suburban life and require special care and caution. I saw my first wild dingo while on an expedition in the Kimberley in Western Australia in 1991 but my first close encounter was a decade later when I visited a dingo sanctuary near Sydney. A dog bounded over to me, jumped up and was so big that its paws rested comfortably on my shoulders as its head nuzzled into my chest. Others in the colony looked as though they would sooner bite off my hand than show me affection.

Their relationship with people has always been a complicated one. Exactly how Aborigines and dingoes benefited each other is still debated. In his book *The Dingo*, Roland Breckwoldt presents a number of possible theories about the friendship between man and dog before the arrival of Europeans in Australia. He says that as hunting aids dingoes may have been more a hindrance than help. More likely, Breckwoldt argues, they were pets, bed-warmers, guard dogs, camp cleaners, a food source, and that 'wild and uncontrollable aspects of the dingo were woven into religious beliefs that underlay the need for order and social stability in Aboriginal society'.

When I set out with South Australian Dog Fence inspector Bill Sandow I had no guarantees that I would be allowed to complete my trip. The South Australian government and the state's Dog Fence Board had given me permission to travel with Sandow only as far as Coober Pedy—less than half of the 2200 kilometres of fence between the Nullarbor and New South Wales. The only time that Sandow could do such a long run in one hit was during the heat of summer, when construction and maintenance work was at a minimum. I had been granted a permit to travel from the New South Wales government but the boss of the Queensland fence had told me not to call him unless I made it through the first two states.

CHAPTER 2

THE WOMBAT FENCE

I had first spoken to Bill Sandow, my travelling companion for the next week, a few months earlier. A man who has spent all his life in the outback, Sandow sounded like a pub poet when he expressed his feelings about the start of the fence. He told me how he had once camped on these cliffs and been disturbed in his sleep by the rumbles and rushes from the blowholes. Now that we were there together, he spoke of his love for this coastline before we set out. 'There's no bloody oil tankers or ships, it's just as it was,' Sandow said. 'If you were here one hundred years ago it would have looked exactly the same except for the bloody Dog Fence.'

I asked if I could cut off the bit of wire sticking out from the end of the fence and hanging over the sea. Sandow looked at me as if I had lost my mind, while I explained that I wanted it as a souvenir. 'No worries,' he said, still baffled, and passed me a pair of wirecutters. 'But do you realise that next week the patrolman could come along here and that piece won't be the beginning of the fence anymore?'

I jumped over the mesh and clambered down to snip off a two-inch section of wire and then another, putting both pieces into my pocket.

Sandow's job requires him to spend twenty-six weeks of the year in the bush, almost always on his own. The year before he was away 200 days and, in the time it took to put 2500 kilometres on the clock of his Commodore sedan, which is garaged in Adelaide, he went through three government four-wheel-drives.

Now he pulled out his .243 rifle from behind his seat and loaded it. 'I sometimes use a .308,' he said as he climbed into the vehicle, 'but that would blow the head off a camel.' The presence of the weapon reminded me that we were not here for the sightseeing. If we came across a dingo then Sandow, like every other person I would meet on my journey, would kill it without hesitation.

On the outside of the fence, the western side where the dingoes are, is a maintenance track that we would follow through to Coober Pedy. Sandow folded back his side vision mirror, rested his chin on his hand and we idled along at ten kilometres per hour. Only a few hundred metres up the track, just as I started wondering how long it would take to drive to Coober Pedy if Sandow's foot didn't press harder on the accelerator, he slammed on the brakes. 'There's bloody three holes in a row.' He climbed out shaking his head. 'That's not like Cyril. He normally never misses a hole.'

Cyril was Anthony Yendall, the patrolman, who had left on his boundary run a few hours earlier. Sandow and I were planning to catch up with him later that morning because, in spite of his head start, the nature of Cyril's job meant that he travelled even more slowly than we did. Sandow tied yellow tape to the fence to mark the holes and then we were on our way again. A quarter of an hour later, and no other holes were found. 'It's holding together pretty well,' Sandow said, 'considering how rusty it is.'

At its beginning on the cliffs the Dog Fence is a remarkably simple barrier—shoulder-high posts slung with wire mesh. Every few hundred metres there were emu and kangaroo-shaped indentations in the netting, where one of the animals had slammed into the wire at full flight. The force of these collisions, at least for the first few dozen times I saw one happen, made me wince. Sometimes the creatures would crash through but most often they quickly bounced back, and in a flurry of fur or feathers would run off in the opposite direction with the gait of a feral muppet. Other times they broke their necks or limbs trying to cross the barrier. Mostly, though, they ran or hopped along the fence until, exhausted, they could travel no further.

After an hour Cyril's truck appeared up ahead. He caught sight of us and stopped to talk to his boss. Sitting in the passenger seat of Cyril's car was John Norwood—known to everyone as Woody. The people of the Ceduna region were beginning to remind me of characters in a Russian novel, where it was necessary to remember both their given name and nickname to follow the story.

I had met both men a couple of days earlier, when Norwood picked me up from my motel in Ceduna and took me to his home at Denial Bay. The bay is a mere indentation in the coast where Flinders had hoped to find a river that he could follow inland. Denial Bay was exactly how I had imagined the fictional White Point in Tim Winton's *Dirt Music* to be. Old fishing shacks sit incongruously beside enormous brick homes, the result of new money flooding into the region causing property prices to skyrocket. On the way there Norwood showed me where the area's original dog fence had once run. Over a century old, it was almost totally overgrown. The barbed wire strands at the top of it and the meshing hanging below were red raw and powdery, and each post was a work of sculpture—sand-blasted, wind-smoothed and sun-dried. Once this old abandoned dog-proof fence went as far as 200 metres into the bay to prevent dingoes paddling around the boundary. The wire that used to hang between the posts in the sea had rusted away long ago.

Norwood and Yendall are great mates, partly because Cyril inherited Woody's patrol along the first 350 kilometres of the fence and partly because of their love of Harley

Davidsons. Norwood managed the fence for twenty years from 1980, saw five Dog Fence inspectors come and go, and starred in around a dozen documentaries. His popularity was due to his natural, rugged manner, his ease with the media and a simple geographical fact. 'This is the only place in Australia,' he told me proudly, 'where the Dog Fence hits the coast.'

I had seen some of these documentaries, which are like a record of Norwood's life; the programs also demonstrate how opinions of the Dog Fence have waxed and waned.

Cyril told a story of how he had woken up one night with whiskers and breath against his sideburns as a dingo sniffed him in his swag. Sandow had experienced a similar close encounter and admitted to feeling very vulnerable while having sweet nothings whispered into his ear by the nation's biggest carnivorous predator. As he lay in his swag Sandow could only hope that the dog did not decide to make a sudden lunge for his jugular.

Two years after his retirement Woody still regularly comes out on a run with Cyril just to enjoy himself. Norwood has a bad back, which he blames on two decades of driving with his head turned hard right to check for holes in the fence. 'Nobody realises what it's like,' Woody told me. 'You drive along and you have your head turned, always looking at the fence and it fucks your neck and back up. When you are patrolling the fence it is like going on a tour on a bus.'

The Dog Fence under Norwood's patrol was revolutionised by electricity. Southern hairy-nosed wombats would dig hundreds of holes through and under the fence, which Woody repeatedly had to fill or block. 'I learned to hate the bastards.' I debated whether to confess to Norwood that my last book had been dedicated to wombats.

Now, out in the bush along the Dog Fence, John Norwood had his hat on and bore a striking resemblance to Richie Cunningham's Dad in 'Happy Days'. Cyril looked like a big scary biker, but as soon as he opened his mouth it was clear that he was a gentle man. Sandow later told me that Yendall was one of his best patrolmen. Cyril offered to make everyone a cup of tea and in a few minutes had a little fire burning with mallee twigs.

Norwood began his working life as a national serviceman in Vietnam and as we sat sipping our tea he told me how he was shot in the chest and lost several close mates. After the war he worked as a stationhand at Frome Downs, which was 2000 kilometres further along the fence and the home of one of the Dog Fence's most talked-about characters—Alec Wilson, a gun-wielding minor movie star. After Frome Downs, Woody worked as a diamond driller before winning the patrolman's contract on the fence.

'I like my own company and I just love the bush,' Norwood told me as we sat on an uprooted mallee log. 'And having nobody looking over my shoulder. You do the job when you feel like it, and as long as it's done properly then everything is OK. It can be pretty bloody boring really—the same fence, the same netting, the same wombats. Patrolmen, including me, put up with eighty years of sticks and stones and sheets of tin, and then some bright spark came along and built an electric fence and it went from 171 holes in a forty-five kilometre section to a couple of holes.'

Yendall drove road trains and farmed before becoming a dogger and patrolman. 'I would rather be out here than at home,' he told me. Unlike many patrolmen Cyril would like to see more of the fence but has not yet met the man who patrols the section after him.

In fact, most boundary riders don't even know the next guy along the wire but they are all part of something so vast, complicated and ambitious as a fence across a continent. In South Australia only Bill Sandow knows all the South Australian components of the Dog Fence. His equivalent in New South Wales is Len Dixon, who also supervises a crew of patrolmen. In Queensland the boss is Jerry Stanley. The three men have only met together once and each runs his operations as a separate entity. But what they have in common is a goal of keeping out dogs.

The fence is a peaceful isolated place and if Australian civilisation has a boundary then I was sitting with three men who help maintain it. The South Australian Dog Fence was different from what I had expected—smaller, slighter, older and more beautiful than the stretch of New South Wales fence I had seen nine years earlier. It is not just about keeping dogs out, the fence is also a lifestyle and I was moving into its orbit. 'If you have never seen the fence you have this vision that there would be all these bloody dogs yapping at it,' Norwood says. 'In twenty years I've not seen any trying to get through.'

Sandow and I said our farewells and headed off at a snail's pace. By mid-afternoon we had travelled only thirty-two kilometres from the coast but had reached our first big landmark—the point where the Dog Fence crosses the Eyre Highway. As we approached the bitumen a ute zoomed over the cattle grid, which is in place to enable vehicles to cross the fence without slowing down. The theory is that a dingo won't cross a grid. Having battled to keep a cunning mini-fox terrier enclosed in my backyard, however, I wasn't convinced that a drooling dog would bat an eyelid at such a barrier and neither are many farmers.

After crossing the road, for a distance of 100 metres on its northern side, the Dog Fence is just 1.5 metres from the Eyre Highway. Hundreds of thousands of Australians pass the fence without even knowing it is there. All they would feel is a bone-rattling chunka-chunk as the grid passes under their car. As we slipped across the highway and made our way further inland it felt as though Sandow and I were doing something illicit. We were heading in a completely different direction from the rest of society—perpendicular to a desolate road rather than along it. In some ways that is how the Dog Fence Board likes it. A constant tension exists between the board's desire for publicity to highlight why graziers should support the fence and the need to keep interest in the structure to a minimum so that tourists do not start using it as the last great four-wheel-drive route across the continent.

I was thinking about all these things when a column of smoke appeared ahead, and as we got closer we realised that a bushfire was burning not far from the fence. While Sandow wondered aloud about what he should do, a yellow paddock basher, a Holden Camira, with four Aborigines on board, came roaring through the scrub and alongside our track. Dust was thrown up in thick plumes and five minutes later the old car disappeared. A few kilometres later Sandow and I saw where the young men had disappeared to—they had pulled open an old gate on the Dog Fence and sped off, leaving it wide open.

Sandow worked to close and rewire the gate and Cyril's voice came on the two-way radio reporting that a whole section of fence on the northern side of the Eyre Highway had been pushed down. Sandow did a U-turn and we met up with Woody and Cyril again. No one was sure when or how the fence was flattened, whether it was the youths in the car or a kangaroo. If an animal had knocked it down, how had we missed it? Even so, Woody and Cyril suspected that it was an animal that did the damage and teased Sandow for failing to spot such a big hole—they probably felt square for his discovery earlier that day. 'Now you have seen,' Sandow said, 'one of the biggest problems we face keeping the fence dog proof out here.' After wombats, Norwood said his biggest battle was closing gates and fixing holes left by Aborigines. But I thought of what someone had said to me in Ceduna: 'Why would they care about this white man's fence that's in their way?'

For the rest of that afternoon the stretch of Dog Fence we travelled along was also an electric wombat-proof fence. The structure had morphed from a rustic work of art into a postmodern, waist-high construction that ran for nearly 100 kilometres. It was hard to believe that a dingo would not simply leap over the barrier, but Bill assured me that unless a dog had a good reason to cross it would not bother. Every eight kilometres Sandow would stop and pull out a voltage meter and check the fence was properly charged. The simplicity of the modern wombat fence makes pastoralists sceptical of its ability to stop dogs. How, leathered graziers ask, can four strands of wire held up by plastic posts possibly keep the dingo on his side of the fence? The old-timers love the big tall fences with strong mallee posts, marsupial netting and barbed wire.

'The theory is as follows,' Sandow explained. 'You need

Bill Sandow. 'Out on the fence you get stupider and stupider, to the point that you see a bird fly by and you fall off your chair with laughter.'

two hundred volts to stop wombats, eight hundred for dogs and two thousand for roos, so you are absolutely frying wombats—giving them one hundred times more charge than they need. It doesn't kill them, but by jeez they think about coming back for a second dose.'

Around dusk an Australian bustard or bush turkey suddenly appeared on the Dog Fence track—a combination of a mini emu, a lordly spiv and the cartoon character Road Runner. Once it saw us, it began running and somehow pulled itself off the ground into the air, just clearing the Dog Fence by a wing flap. For local Aborigines the bird is the central character in one of the Nullarbor Plain's most important songlines—the Bush Turkey songline.

At 7.30 pm, after filling our water tanks with rainwater stored at a shed owned by the local Dog Fence Board, we pulled into a cleared area sheltered by a stand of mallee and set up camp. The nightly fire is one of the most important things to Bill. Sometimes he even makes two—a big roaring one for warmth and a smaller one to cook on.

'I always get my fire going,' he told me as he dragged over a big dead mallee log and propped a pile of broken branches beside it. 'Then I dig a hole for the coals. I wrap my spuds and onions in foil and put them in the hole. Then you've got half an hour to have a beer before you put your meat on. I've got to have a balanced diet because I spend so much time in the bush.'

Opening a can of peas and carrots and without a trace of irony, Bill said, 'You've got to have your vegies. My doctor tells me to lay off the meat so I said I would only eat meat six times a week. He told me I needed to drink more fluids so I said I would have three beers a night instead of two.'

Every evening at eight he is also required to ring through on his satellite phone to his boss in Adelaide to let him know he is safe. There was no moon—something for which Sandow was happy because it meant it would be fully dark. 'When there's a full moon out here you have to shift your swag and sleep in the shadow of the trees.'

After our meal Sandow talked of shooting stars that leave trails of colour from one side of the sky to the other, of strange planes that fly in odd patterns at extremely high altitude. He explained how he loved lying in his swag and watching out for satellites. Once he had seen a space shuttle dock at the new international space station. 'It was like watching two dots chase each other across the sky,' he said in a voice full of awe. Sandow leads such an isolated existence that he found out about the September 11 terrorist attacks four days later.

We both woke up just before dawn, absolutely soaked by a heavy dew that had drifted in from the Southern Ocean. As I scrabbled out of my sleeping bag, I could see the planet Mercury to the east. I had slept badly, however, and I felt slimy and uncomfortable. Breakfast was bacon, eggs and toast. I also brewed up a coffee. Already, after only twenty-four hours together, Sandow and I had settled into a routine that seemed to suit us both. He cooked, and I cleaned up the mess.

From our camp the fence ran towards the east, parallel to the coast. Two days earlier I had, by chance, explored this section with sheep farmer Ricky Hammat and camel adventurer Chris Richards.

I had heard rumours of Richards' adventures and tracked him down the morning after I arrived in Ceduna. He invited me to visit him at Hammat's property the day before Sandow and I set out. It was hot, still and uncomfortable. Sweat ran down from beneath my hat, down my face and into my beard. Camel bells slung around the necks of the ten hobbled, terrified, wild beasts in front of me were jangling so incessantly that their noise began to feel like a form of torture. Dust was everywhere. Flies buzzed around my face, down my mouth, up my nose, into the corners of my eyes and into my ears.

The young man I was talking to, twenty-eight-year-old Chris Richards, seemed oblivious to my discomfort. His face was hidden by the shadow cast from a big fur-felt hat and a thick and dirty beard as rough as scrub. He was wearing a heavy woollen jumper and his eyes had a haunted, sunken cast. Richards had recently been close to death. He had walked over 1500 kilometres from Perth to Hammat's yards with three camels. On the way he had eaten lizards and even an echidna to survive, and quenched his thirst from muddy puddles. Train drivers on the Nullarbor's Great Southern Railway line, which Richards had followed, tossed him newspapers and scraps as they passed. He had been lucky enough to run into Ricky Hammat and his wife Tanya, who offered him the chance to recuperate on their property. Soon after, a chest infection turned into pneumonia.

Like me, Richards wanted to travel the entire 5400-kilometre length of the Dog Fence. His journey was a re-creation of nineteenth-century camel expeditions and would take at least a year to complete. The trek was significant for another reason—until fifty years ago camels carried the Dog Fence inspectors.

Before Richards could leave he had ten wild camels to break in. They were big Simpson Desert males that had probably never seen a human until they were caught near Coober Pedy. Each one cost $2000 to transport to Ceduna. Turning these terrified bulls into pack animals, however, was not Richards' biggest problem. So far he had been unable to find anyone to accompany him on his trip, and with four tonnes of gear to pack and then unpack each day he was facing a near-impossible task.

Water was also a serious worry—for the first 1000 kilometres he needed to plan for the possibility that he would not find a single drop. A third fear was other wild camels. Even though his bulls had all been castrated, Richards had been told they would still be a target for sex-starved desert males known to mistake cut bulls for cows.

Steel-jawed dog traps are also set right along the fence. 'If one steps in one of those I'm going to have to administer a lead aspirin pretty quickly,' Richards said. I had left my notebook on top of a post and as each of the camels passed they stopped to sniff it. 'They are very smart. They never forget if you do something mean to them. They will patiently wait until you are off-guard and then kick you or bite you,' Richards said. 'Putting your life into the hands of ten wild camels *is* pretty crazy.'

At that moment I turned around to see Ricky Hammat's face as he bent to look through a gap in the timber yards. I walked over and shook his hand. 'You wanna cup of coffee or something?' he asked.

We talked for a bit and then Hammat offered to take Chris and me up to the fence for a drive. It was 11 am. He pulled out an esky and filled it with a case of beer before we headed due north for half an hour, in which time we drank two beers each. I don't usually drink during the day and the alcohol went straight to my head. When we reached the fence Hammat cut the motor.

'The fence is an excellent thing in every respect,' he told me. 'It protects my sheep, it's a great place to come with mates and have a party and it's a good road to use for a drive to the beach.'

On the other side of the fence was the Yumbarra Conservation Park. 'We come out here and have a barbecue— I don't know what else you would use a national park for. I would much rather buy a carton of beer and fifty bucks worth of diesel and come out here than spend three times that at a disco in Adelaide,' Hammat said. 'It doesn't matter how much noise they make or what fools they make of themselves.'

Out along the fence is also a favourite place that Hammat and his family go to collect native peaches from the quandong tree (*Santalum acuminatum*). The quandong is one of the few native species that has made it as a mainstream bush tucker food and it could become as famous as the macadamia. Recent research has shown that the fruits—bright red and fleshy—have twice the vitamin C of an orange. For desert Aborigines the tree is a staple of life and culture. The stones of the fruit contain extremely nutritious kernels that are 25 per cent protein and 70 per cent oil and, according to ethno-botanist Peter Latz, a paste made from the ground seeds is used as a liniment for general ailments. Hammat handed me a couple of the stones, which are spherical with a surface texture somewhere between a walnut and a peach pit. Jiggling them, it didn't surprise me at all to learn that Aboriginal children use them for marbles.

Hammat pulled twenty cents from his pocket and flipped it high against the blue sky. 'Heads we go east and tails we go west.'

We followed the fence westwards, stopping at each steel-jawed trap to see what was caught. The jaws of the trap are wiped with strychnine-laced grease so that when an animal is slammed tight by the steel, it licks its wound and dies faster. Without the poison a trapped dog can survive for days and often will chew its leg off to escape. The traps are buried under the sand and surrounded by a three-walled mound of mallee logs. Years worth of skeletons and decaying wildlife surround the traps. Every animal that feasts on carrion is drawn to these trap sites. A crow was in one trap that we passed, a cat in another and there were several foxes. Then we stopped beside a trap with a decomposed dingo, circled by several dead shingleback lizards. Shinglebacks are not meat-eaters but may scavenge when food is scarce. It was likely they had eaten some of the dead dog's stomach contents.

'Can I give you some advice?' Hammat said, casting a serious and worried glance at my feet. 'Don't wear sandals. Out here it's too dangerous. Get yourself some boots.'

He explained that sometimes a dog drags a trap away from where it was set, without triggering it. Sandals or boots, either way it seemed to me that if my ankle got stuck in a trap my leg would be a mess.

A few kilometres further on we came to an old tin shed that the local footy club uses for an annual all-night drinking party. Another ten kilometres and we reached what looked like a rubbish tip. 'This belongs to the Prices,' Hammat said. 'The old man is not too keen on visitors so we won't stay long.' There were rows of the rusted-out bodies of 1940s trucks and cars beside piles of prefabricated building parts. Some of the material had been collected from Maralinga after the nuclear tests of the 1950s.

As we were about to leave, a Toyota ute came into the clearing. Hammat introduced me to the driver, Phoompy

Price. After I shook Phoompy's hand I noticed a thumbnail-sized spike of saltbush stuck into the front driver's-side tyre. I bent over to have a look. 'Don't touch the fuckin' cunt,' Phoompy told me. 'I am fuckin' hopin' to get another fuckin' few weeks out of that fuckin' tyre.' Never before had I heard a man who swore as much as Phoompy.

He accepted a beer from Hammat. It turned out that the two were mates and had even completed an explosives course together. After their training, a party was organised out near the fence so a drum of TNT could be detonated. The fuse was too short but luckily no one got hurt.

Phoompy looked hungover. When he threw his cigarette butt on the ground, ants swarmed all over it. 'What were you drinking last night, Phoompy?' Hammat asked. I too imagined that the ants had been attracted by the sweetness of spirits. 'Nothin', mate, I was off the grog yesterday but I had a fuckin' gutful the night before.'

Hammat wanted to show me an old rockhole and asked Phoompy for directions. Phoompy crouched down and began drawing lines and tracks in the sand. He drew a great looping ring that was the shape of an elongated bubble about to burst. By the end of the mapmaking there was a pattern not unlike an Aboriginal sand painting.

Euria Rockhole has existed for thousands of years and in 1904 work was undertaken to increase its water storage. The big exposed slab of rock was buttressed by concreted

Wild dogs caught in strychnine-laced traps are like a magnet to other wildlife, which is in turn also killed by the poison.

stonework which funnelled rainwater into an enlarged natural depression. In its original state, when full it held around 2000 litres of water, which was crucial to the survival of hundreds of generations of Aborigines—a sobering thought when I consider that my water tank at home holds 6000 litres and is easily emptied if it doesn't rain.

The controversial writer and anthropologist Daisy Bates claimed that the local Aborigines were cannibals and that Euria was the scene of 'many a human oven'. In 1938, in her most important book, *The Passing of the Aborigines*, Bates wrote:

> When a fight ended fatally the victim was cooked and shared, unless he was an important or very old member of a group, then he would be carried back for burial to his own ground...When their little growing boys showed signs of decline or weakness, a baby brother or sister was killed and cooked, laid on its face upon the hot cinders, and the fat of the baby was rubbed all over the weakling boy, and he ate of its flesh in the morning and the evening until it was all finished, and he had become strong again, and grew fat and big.

Bates' claim of cannibalism at Euria has been largely discredited, and no one knows exactly what rituals took place on this spot. Nevertheless, Euria is an example of cultural history lost.

Other things would be lost during this journey too. Three months after my meeting with Richards he made it another forty kilometres along the Dog Fence. Two female backpackers who joined him at the last moment abandoned the expedition and headed south to Ceduna. For three days Richards sat with the beasts he had spent his life savings on. It would be impossible for him to go on alone. Richards pulled out his .303 rifle, shot all ten of his camels in the head and left them to rot in the scrub beside the fence.

Sandow and I now passed the spot where I had met Phoompy. As we reached the 150-kilometre mark the wombat fence morphed back to the antique Dog Fence, and spinifex, the emblem of the desert, began to appear. Aborigines use the plant's resin as a glue and children make miniature spears out of its sharp leaves and play a game that involves spiking flies.

Another of Sandow's important rituals is his mid-morning orange. We stopped the car near Ross and Yvonne Borlace's property, Ryreem, and while Sandow spoke to his boss Michael Balharry and ate his orange, I started to hear a steady hissing sound. We had a flat tyre.

It is a golden rule for Sandow to travel with two spare tyres. We had hundreds of kilometres of sand dunes to cross and in summer, when dunes turn viscous and slippery, this can mean chewing through enormous volumes of diesel. We needed to go back to Ceduna.

In that spot we also saw our first budgerigars. In December 1989, after a massive heatwave with temperatures regularly in the mid-40s, the budgies came in to Ryreem from the desert seeking shade and water. For a fortnight they raked up the dead birds and carted them away in 20-litre drums. The birds covered the surface of their water tank and even tried to drink spilled oil and break into aviaries to get at water.

In the mid-afternoon we drove off the Dog Fence and an hour later we were back in Ceduna. I began to feel as though I had not yet reached an escape velocity that would finally fling me away from there.

While Sandow filled his long-range fuel tanks and repaired the tyre, a man came up and said 'Gidday'. It was Kym Trewartha, a member of the Dog Fence Board whom I had met the day before when Sandow and I headed to the start of the fence. I felt I was becoming a part of Ceduna. On my second and third meetings with these people conversation

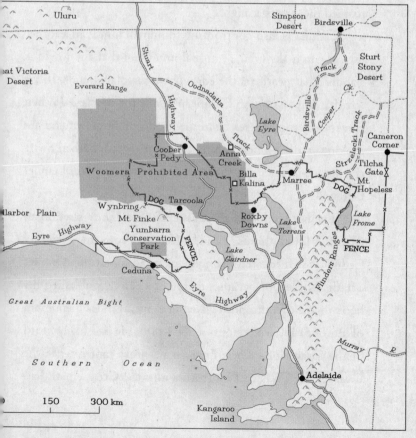

The South Australian Dog Fence.

was easy—we knew each other, we had the fence in common and I was with Sandow, a respected visitor to the community.

This was my fourth departure from the town in four days. No matter how much the world changes Ceduna will always be a frontier town. Race relations there are as raw as a bad sunburn. I had been surprised by both the racist remarks I had heard there and the reason for them—dozens of Aborigines begging, destitute and drunk outside the pub. A three-metre steel fence surrounded my motel and children roamed the streets at night.

Ceduna is also confronting to human minds in another way. It can make even a rational mind feel that the world is flat and that nearby is the edge where the planet ends. It has left that impression on European minds for centuries. When you stare across the sea from the shores of the town you are looking at a bay where, nearly 300 years ago, Jonathan Swift chose to exile his great fictional adventurer, Captain Lemuel Gulliver.

The last section of the classic *Gulliver's Travels* is set on an island, Houyhnhnms Land, offshore from modern-day Ceduna. Swift located the home of a race of utopian horses off the Nullarbor because, in 1726, when he published his book of bizarre, imagined adventures, it was in the penumbra of Europe's known regions of the world. He had likely heard of the voyages of Francis Thijssen a century earlier, when the *Golden Seahorse* was cast by storms into the Great Australian

Bight. Gulliver 'arrived' on the island after being outcast and set adrift by his fellow sailors. St Peter Island—Houyhnhnms Land—is over the horizon.

Soon we were back along the fence and I felt like a stone that has been spun round and round on a string then finally released. Phoompy, Woody, Cyril, Trewartha, Hammat, Richards and Ceduna were disappearing beyond the rear-view mirror's horizon at 15 kilometres per hour.

We would not see another human being on the fence for the next 800 kilometres.

CHAPTER 3
WYNBRING

As we headed into the Great Victoria Desert it was obvious that we were driving along an early section of the Dog Fence. We were traversing the boundary of Puereba National Park.

Fences in this part of the world are so old and diverse that near the town of Port Lincoln, south-east of Ceduna, in the Koppio Smithy Museum, is a vast barbed wire and dog trap collection. I spent an evening with Leon Dobbins who, with his father Bob, has amassed nearly 1500 of the world's 2000 varieties of barbed wire. The pair began searching for odd types of wire from old, redundant dog fences littered across the state then became so obsessed that today they own everything from a full roll of unused razor wire from Pentridge Prison to a section of barb from the Berlin Wall.

After meeting with Leon I could not look at an old fence without wondering what I *wasn't* able to see because of my ignorance about the evolution of wire and fencing technology. One example is the humble star picket, patented in the 1920s, which I had thought one of the most mundane objects ever invented. It is, however, critical in keeping the Dog Fence standing. Patrolmen also call the pickets 'droppers'. A true dropper is not stuck into the ground but is used to keep the strands of wire between posts apart. By helping provide tension to a fence, star pickets and droppers reduce the number of posts required. The Dobbins family owns 150 different types of dropper—each with its own story of invention. Today only one is in common use—the distinctive steel post with the formal name 'Star ® Picket'.

Another metal milestone crucial to the Dog Fence is the steel-jawed trap and the Dobbins have dozens. They range from one that hangs from a tree, with spikes that slam into a dingo's muzzle when it jumps for bait, to a 'mantrap' for catching Aborigines.

We were leaving the mallee country and the sand was changing colour to red. Spinifex had replaced saltbush as the dominant ground cover and we saw our first dead camel, which resembled a piece of furniture covered tightly with a sheet. In 2001, following a month of temperatures in the forties, herds of camels had swept out of the desert and died of thirst and starvation when they hit the fence. We came to our first big sand dunes and I commented on how mountainous they looked. 'You wait until tomorrow around

Steel-jawed dog traps are rarely used in Australia—except on the Dog Fence.

Lake Everard,' Sandow responded. 'When you get to the top of one of those sand dunes you can look to the horizon and see a straight line over the dunes where the track follows the fence. When you get to the next horizon you see exactly the same sight all over again.'

At 6.30 we parked at the bottom of a sand dune to set up camp. Sandow hates the wind and always sleeps in the lee of his four-wheel-drive. The back of his vehicle is full of his camping gear—his swag, his fold-up bed and chairs. The food we had purchased at Ceduna was in his car fridge, in a special metal box. I had decided to travel light and for me setting up meant only throwing out my ground mat and sleeping bag. Five minutes after we stopped Bill and I were enjoying a cold beer, moving our chairs with the shadows to avoid the sun, which held its bite to the last second before it dropped over the horizon.

At dusk I went for a walk northwards along the fence. The closer I got to the structure and the further I walked away from camp, the smaller I felt. The fence was electric so there was no way of crossing to the other side—I was blocked off from south-eastern Australia just like every other creature. I began to feel a new respect for the fence. I understood why a dog wouldn't try to cross without a good reason. I thought of the words written in *Holding the Line*, a history of the South Australian Dog Fence Board:

> Perhaps it is preferable to think of the fence as a 'line in the sand' that the board has drawn to defend. The fortification of the 'line' depends on the needs and conditions at each length and location and the extent to which trapping and baiting have cleared the enemy from each area.

That night we ate lamb chops, baked potatoes and tinned vegetables. Bill has a big fluorescent light that he plugs into the back of his vehicle. As soon as it was switched on masses of beetles came swarming around our camp. The dishwashing tub had a film of water on its base and was quickly filled with hundreds of insects of every shape, size and colour—some possibly unknown to science.

After dinner I filled half of my billy with some of our precious water and heated it on Sandow's giant fire. At 9 pm it was still light enough to see and twilight, which continues until the sun has travelled 20 degrees beyond the horizon, did not seem to end until 9.30. I carried the billy fifty metres from the fire and had my first wash on the Dog Fence. Sandow was right—even just another fifty kilometres inland

Sandow's camp. 'When you are older you can sit out here and enjoy having a beer on your own.'

and the stars were much brighter, as if a filter had been taken away. I lay on top of my sleeping bag and felt stoned. The hard ground was warm and I felt pinned to the Earth.

Everything about the day had made me feel small. And now the stars were so bright that each time I blinked I could still see them. I felt as though the universe was not just something all around me, but that it was inside me as well.

I lay there looking up at the stars through the desert vegetation—there were so many that they looked like little electric lights which had been strung up on every branch and twig of every shrub and tree. A micro-bat hunting insects swooped down close to my head. It was hardly bigger than a moth but flew with great agility and speed. I could hear the ticking of my watch and then a whole chorus of sounds erupted around my bed: crickets in the spinifex a few metres away, a dingo yapping, a screech that was probably a wombat. Twigs were snapping, the ground was cooling and it seemed that the universe is layer upon layer of throbbing, unstoppable noise. A shooting star flew like a streamer across the north-west, leaving a trail of greens and blues that stretched from the top of the sky almost to the horizon. Then I smiled at something Sandow had said earlier: 'As long as you can fart you are still alive.' Noises are life, and we make sounds so other things know we exist. I wanted to lie there awake and watch the universe but the next thing I knew Sandow was cracking up bits of kindling and getting our breakfast fire going. 'The sleeps get better as you go along,' he told me over our bacon and eggs. I described my strange thoughts of the night before. 'The only sound I usually hear at night,' he responded, 'is the fridge cutting in and out.'

Straight out of camp we passed a patch of desert oak forest. Once these trees would have provided an important food to the Mirning people who lightly roasted the cones to release green seeds. At times the cones also produce a sweet, white substance which is eaten on the spot or soaked in water. The roots were also a good source of water for Aboriginal people. Scientist Peter Latz says at least seven plant species were used as a water source by desert dwellers. In his book *Bushfires and Bushtucker* Latz writes:

> The roots are located either by the presence of fine cracks in the ground or by investigatory digging near the trunk. Once broken off they can easily be pulled from the ground, especially if found in sandy areas, and then broken into metre-long pieces. These lengths are then placed into a container, ensuring that the ends initially closest to the trunk are placed downwards. If the water does not immediately seep out of the roots a burning stick is applied to their distal ends to encourage movement. The better plants supply enough water for two to three people from several bundles of roots, even if the liquid is rather thick and sappy.

Using a clever combination of utilising water-storing tree hollows, collecting dew with bundles of grass, and consuming fleshy leaves, the swollen roots of lilies and bush potatoes, desert Aborigines thrived in what to European eyes seems a waterless environment.

Latz says the desert oaks remind him of hairy triffids. To Aborigines they were important characters in songs and stories. Desert oak timber made strong clubs and heavy fighting spears. The ash was added to the native plant pituri, a shrub containing nicotine which was traded throughout central Australia; the ash aids in the absorption of the drug.

Past the desert oaks Sandow climbed out to test the voltage of the electric Dog Fence. He pushed a lever to shut down the power and went to climb over. The moment he swung his leg over his whole body jolted with the shock of electricity. 'Jeeessuuss!' he shouted. 'That gets you going in the morning. That got me right up through the shoulder blades, but my backache's gone.'

Everyone driving in the desert has a two-way radio. Sandow has his on scan all day—mainly as a safety defence against people illegally driving along the Dog Fence track. Every fence inspector and boundary rider has stories of near misses with tourists speeding along the track. Sandow has learnt that when four-wheel-drivers travel in convoy they never stop using the radio to talk to each other. By tuning in he can let anyone coming from the other direction know that he too is on the fence.

The radio also gives a glimpse into daily life across central Australia. As we passed Nuckulla Hill—a 264-metre-high, mallee-covered outpost of the Everard Range (where explorer Charles Sturt discovered the sublime flower, Sturt's desert pea)—a man's voice came over the radio complaining about a mouse plague in his home. His wife had caught five the night before. Another man called Bob replied, 'I'll bring some stuff around to kill 'em. I'll just leave it on the verandah.'

'The only problem is that the little dog is off the leash and I'm not there,' came the response. 'He won't eat that shit, will he?'

'No worries, mate. I'll leave it in a container and you can sprinkle it where it's safe.'

'Thanks, Bob.'

From our vantage point on the western extreme of the Everard Ranges there was only the fence, the track and our vehicle to indicate the presence of humans. This community doesn't show itself until you are right on top of it or eavesdrop on a radio conversation. The exchange with Bob provided an interesting insight into the way people out here view dogs. Many properties in central Australia have a house dog, usually a little terrier that leads a privileged life indoors. The next rung down are the working dogs, mostly kelpies, that muster during the day and are chained up in dusty yards at night. At the bottom of the heap is the dingo. Few people care if he spends days in a steel-jawed trap or is poisoned by strychnine.

By the time we stopped for our morning orange it was already so hot that breathing 'unconditioned' air was difficult. Some tufts of cloud were on the horizon and Sandow feared we might hit thunderstorms in the next couple of days. He promised we would be camping under heavy skies that evening. Soon the last of the electrified wire was behind us and we were back along some of the tattiest sections of the fence in all of South Australia. 'The fence may look pretty ratty but it's perfectly dog-proof,' Sandow said. 'I don't reckon this section is that old. It was built around 1945.'

In front of us was a 400-kilometre-long stretch of huge dunes, some up to twenty metres high that we had to cross. The closer we got to midday the harder the travelling became. When sand is heated it behaves more like quicksand and vehicles can get stuck very easily. Even Sandow had to concentrate to climb the Everard sand dunes. To get through meant dropping the transmission into low four then accelerating as many revs as the car could handle by starting as far back as possible from the dune. On the big hills Sandow would aim to get his four-wheel-drive as high as he could, making two wheel tracks close to the summit of the dune where the sand was compacted. He would then reverse down and run up again, this time following the tracks where he had already packed down the sand. Each time his revs would carry him a little further towards the top. The worst possible thing that can happen is that you run out of revs with the front tyres on one side of the summit and the rear tyres on the other.

'If you get stuck at the top of the sand dune you're fucked,' Sandow said as his revs only just cleared us over the top of one hill. 'If you stop on top you can't reverse back, you can't drive forward and you can't winch yourself off.'

Sandow carries a compressor to re-pump his tyres in case he is forced to let them down to get more traction on dunes. He has also had times when there was nothing else for it but to wait until the cool of the evening when the sand becomes firmer and the four-wheel-drive can move again. This trip Sandow had to be in Coober Pedy in four days so there was no time to get stuck anywhere. With his deadline in mind he hit each dune as if he were running into the surf with a boogie board. In deep sand the vehicle seemed like a boat paddling up the face of a wave.

The dunes were in fact the perfect habitat for two animals that I was keen to see. I had a chance of spotting a thorny devil—these lizards are relatively common but are very small and terrifically well camouflaged. The other creature is one of the most enigmatic of all Australian mammals. To see a marsupial mole is the naturalist's equivalent of winning a lottery. Only a handful of Europeans have seen one in the wild.

By lunchtime, even with the airconditioning, my thermometer said it was 33 degrees Celsius inside the car and in the mid-forties outside. This was the first time Sandow had ever had a thermometer in the vehicle and he couldn't take his eyes off it, exclaiming every half an hour that if we were getting these readings on what he said was a mild day then he must have gone through some damned hot days—temperatures at least ten degrees hotter in the shade. 'There was one day that I was drinking a bottle of water every hour and I don't think I took a leak all day,' he said. 'The heat was just sapping it out of me.'

One of my jobs was to make the midday sandwiches. The temperature combined with a constant dry wind made the bread feel like toast no matter how quickly I buttered it, slapped in the filling and ate.

The vegetation was beginning to change again, from mallee to mulga, and the spinifex was replaced by saltbush. Mulga was the cornerstone of survival for desert Aborigines. Peter Latz calculates that, even in an average year, one five-hectare stand of mulga can provide a month's supply of seed for one hundred people, which is more than a quarter of their food needs. The job of sorting the seeds, also known as yandying, fell to the women, which, according to Latz 'involves a very intricate and skilful rotating and jiggling movement of an elongated wooden dish (a coolamon) which separates objects of differing density and/or surface characteristics.'

The yandying technique has been so perfected that women in a Western Australian community were once asked to yandy mineral sands after an initial batch was deemed too impure for commercial use. 'This deceptively simple method of separating particles of different densities,' Latz writes, 'proved to be more efficient than any complicated method that modern technology had been able to develop.'

The desert plants in front of me looked more dead than alive. As if reading my thoughts Sandow said, 'She's hard country out here.' It was as if we were crossing the floor of a dry ocean. There was nothing but sand with tortured, stunted trees sticking out of it. After lunch we passed what is the northernmost colony of southern hairy-nosed wombats on Earth. The warren was active—I could see dung and scratchings—and there was clear damage to the Dog Fence. Sandow advocates the eradication of this outpost of wombats, but to do the job he needs the help of local pastoralists and removing the marsupials is not their greatest priority because the fence is the government's problem.

Late that afternoon Mount Finke came into view. John McDouall Stuart, the first European to see it, made an optimistic approach on 6 August 1858. 'It seems to be very high, and I expect something good will be the result of our visit to it tomorrow.' Yet twenty-four hours later, the second night Stuart's party was without water, the explorer was depressed. 'I almost give up hopes of a good country; this is very disheartening, after all that I have done to find it...I got on one of the lower spurs of Mount Finke to see what was before me. The prospect is gloomy in the extreme! I could see a long distance but nothing met the eye save a dense scrub as *black and dismal as midnight*.' Stuart climbed it again at dawn but in the morning he was enshrouded by mist. From the lonely explorer's eyrie he recorded the view as 'a fearful country'.

Ernest Giles climbed the peak in April 1875. As we had, Giles and his party travelled over hellish sand dunes, so 'steep and high that all our animals were in a perfect lather of sweat'. At first light on 3 April, Giles started to climb Mount Finke:

> I could not help thinking it was the most desolate heap on the face of the earth, having no water or places that could hold it. The elevation of this eminence was over 1000 feet above the surrounding country, and over 2000 feet above the sea. The country visible from its summit was still enveloped in dense scrubs in every direction, except on a bearing a few degrees north of east, where some low ridges appeared. I rode my horse, Chester, many miles over the wretched stony slopes at the foot of this mountain, and tied him up to trees while I walked to its summit, and into gullies and crevices innumerable, but no water rewarded my efforts...After wasting several hours in a fruitless search for water, we left the wretched mount, and steered away for the ridges I had seen from its summit.

Giles was back at Finke on 20 June. He was about to undertake one of the last great challenges of Australian exploration—a crossing of the continent from east to west. Winter in the desert can greatly lift a traveller's spirits—days are fresh and mild, insects are in abeyance and water is not sucked out of human flesh as it is in summer:

> The weather, now cool and agreeable, was so different from that which I had previously experienced upon this dreadful mount...the desolate region around was enjoying for a few weeks only, a slight respite from the usual fiery temperature of the climate of this part of the world; but even now the nature of the country was so terrible and severe, the sandhills so high, and the scrub so thick, that all the new members of the party expressed their astonishment that we had ever got out of it alive.

I wished we could have made the ascent to see if Giles' cairn was still in place, but Sandow was working and the clouds were threatening—as he had promised at breakfast. The hardest desert country was still ahead of us and he had his appointment at Coober Pedy. Later I learned from a retired Northern Territory policeman, Ian Holland, who climbed Finke in 1999, that the cairn was still there, and was a spectacular piece of stonework.

That night we camped five kilometres south of the Great Southern Railway line and five metres from the Dog Fence.

At 8 pm it was still 35 degrees and there was not a breath of wind. The humidity was so low that my hydrometer could not detect it. As soon as we stopped, flies swarmed all over me—especially around my eyes, ears and a cut on my finger. Bill too was smothered by the insects—there were so many that they gave his head a soft focus. 'They'll disappear when the sun goes down,' he promised unconvincingly.

In spite of the heat, Bill prepared a fire, pulling down an entire dead tree and building a pile of twigs and branches beside it. Without any paper or kindling he said he was going to use an old bushman's trick to start the fire. I thought anything from a flint to a magnifying glass was possible; instead I watched him retrieve his can of WD40. He knelt beside the fallen tree, pressed the aerosol button and flicked his lighter in front of the jet of gas. A blast of flame, like a flamethrower, erupted for a few seconds and our fire was quickly roaring. I hoped the smoke would discourage the flies. This problem is not a new one. Giles wrote:

> They infest the whole air, they seem to be circum-ambient; we can't help eating, drinking and breathing flies; they go down our throats in spite of our teeth, and we wear them all over our bodies; they creep up one's clothes and die, and others go after them to see what they died of. The instant I inhale a fly it acts as an emetic. And if Nature abhors a vacuum, she or at least

my nature, abhors these wretches more, for the moment I swallow one a vacuum is instantly produced.

'The reason you've got so many flies on you,' Sandow told me, 'is because you had a wash last night.' An hour later it was pitch-black and the last few flies slowed to a pace that made them easy swatting targets. Finally there were none at all and we could eat our T-bone steak, baked potatoes and tinned peas in peace. I washed again and went to sleep under deep, tufty grey clouds.

The flies were back early and it was clear that this new day would be even hotter than the one before. What was I doing? Ahead of me was still 5000 kilometres of Dog Fence. What was the point of travelling the length of it? When I told Sandow of my doubts he said that was exactly why young people did not make good patrolmen. 'When you're young you can stand the fence for a while. But by the time you're forty you've lost your zest for living and you can stand it for longer. When you're older you can enjoy sitting out here and having a beer on your own.'

Sandow asked whether I could hear a train coming. I couldn't but about five minutes later a dull rumble rolled through, then passed as slowly as it arrived. At its loudest I could detect the sounds of an engine and even the clackety-clack of a long train. 'We're out in the middle of the desert, hundreds of kilometres from the closest four-wheel-drive or homestead,' he said, turning the eggs and bacon, 'and the only sound you can hear is a train.'

I walked over to the fence, aware that it marks an important ecological boundary—the furthest extreme of sheep country. To the west of where I was standing there was not another fence for thousands of kilometres—well into the agricultural lands of Western Australia. Yet that did not mean there were no other boundaries.

In a speech in 2002, archaeologist Scott Cane explained that the land tenure rules of the Aborigines of the Great Victoria Desert are sophisticated and strong:

> If you are a Spinifex Person, the place where you were born—or more correctly the place where you first touch the ground—is the heart of your country...But country is also defined by the place where her [sic] dried umbilical cord fell off after birth. Now because people are nomadic—water holes dry up and food runs out—families move. So that location—where your cord falls off—could be anywhere.

Back on the track and after a few minutes' drive we reached the intersection of the Dog Fence and the train tracks. An agreement to build the railway was struck between the federal, South Australian and Western Australian governments in 1907. The idea was to build it between Tarcoola and Kalgoorlie, enabling travel from one side of Australia to the other. The survey work was completed in 1912 and the construction in 1917. Each of the sidings was named after an Australian prime minister, except for Ooldea, which retained its Aboriginal name because of local opposition.

But by the end of the nineteenth century Aborigines had followed explorers like Warburton, Giles, Forrest and Maurice into European civilisation. According to Bates, those that remained in the desert were terrified of camels, which they called *windinjirri*. The white man was *waijela*. Bafflingly, the *waijela* killed the kangaroos but left the meat to rot and kept only the skins. He took over the waterholes and allowed *windinjirri* to drink all the water. Then *waijela* started paying Aborigines in cash or kind—usually either alcohol or tobacco. Low-life whites devoured Aboriginal women as hungrily as they appropriated other resources. The fabric of desert culture was shredded by disease, brutality, disenfranchisement and addiction. The railway line cut a devastating wound across cultural groups that had survived in the desert for tens of thousands of years.

Word of mouth spread and desert people travelled hundreds of kilometres to Ooldea, Wynbring and Tarcoola like moths to light, attracted by food and drink. Those aware of the evils besetting their communities hoped that the white man would build the railway and leave. But it is only in recent years that ghost towns like Wynbring, which once housed railway workers, have been bulldozed into deep pits. Travellers can look out on the desert from a buffet car, drinking champagne in airconditioned comfort, and have no idea of the cultural devastation that a few thousand kilometres of steel tracks, sleepers and stones has wrought.

Cane says, however, it took generations for many Spinifex people to learn that their country had been settled by white people. 'They lived through two world wars and didn't even know they had happened...They saw the tracks of the Indian Pacific railway crossing the Nullarbor, which they thought were the actual tracks of the Wati Wanampi—the terrifying water snake, the so-called rainbow serpent.'

To stop dogs crossing the fence at the railway line, six enormous, medieval-looking plates are laid down on the rocky ballast between the tracks—three are covered in thousands of nails and three have arrow-shaped slices of metal. The only way a dingo could get to the inside of the fence would be to tightrope-walk along the shiny tracks. Undoubtedly, though, some wild dogs are unstoppable, and even Sandow acknowledges that fact. 'Nothing will stop a dingo if he's really determined. You could build a brick wall along the whole Dog Fence and the dingo will build a ladder to get himself up or throw a rope over. This is a barrier fence meant to keep most of the dogs out. We keep ninety-nine per cent outside the fence and that's enough for the guys inside to make a living.'

For the next forty kilometres the fence heads westwards, closely following the train tracks. A service road runs along the Great Southern Railway line for its entire length. Sandow once encountered a Japanese cyclist on this road, making his own epic journey, and his scariest moment in five years of inspecting the fence occurred along this forty-kilometre section. He was waved over by two men in a hire truck. Both were acting extremely oddly. They were covered in tattoos and from the moment Sandow laid eyes on them he knew that his life was in their hands. The truck, he suspected, was stolen. The men had no idea where they were or where they were going. Sandow calmly showed them a map and gave them directions and then left as quickly as he could. That night he drove into the desert sand dunes until he was beyond their reach.

Along this same stretch Sandow's predecessor, John Cook, once found a man who had lost an arm in a train accident and had to nurse him for a full day until help arrived. John Norwood discovered some German tourists stuck in a sand dune near the railway maintenance track. They had been bogged for six days and did not realise that the four-wheel-drive facility on their car had not been activated. As soon as Norwood turned their hubs and showed them how to drive out of the sand they were away.

The maintenance track is a wide, well-graded road and on this day the only other creatures we shared it with were emus. Two of them ran ahead at 40 kilometres per hour. Over the next month emus would run in front of me every day but for now it was an exhilarating novelty. The only way to pass them was to wait until they either exhausted themselves or the fence had a sharp turn and the birds kept running straight ahead. Their stamina and pace were amazing.

Long, muscly legs pounded the sand, kicking up stones that flicked back and threatened to break the windscreen. Their gait reminded me of the 400-metre World and Olympic champion, Michael Johnson: the upper body straight and relaxed while the legs worked like pistons. Every now and then they would turn their tiny heads around as if checking how the runners in the other lanes were faring. Their eyes had a look of focused terror yet it was hard to understand why they didn't just peel off the track and disappear into the scrub.

The curator of vertebrates at the Queensland Museum, Steve Van Dyck, says it is easy to 'conclude that their heads contain one of the more modest achievements in the evolution of avian grey matter. But away from fences and in their own domain, wild emus are nothing short of spectacular...the imagination can be fired by no more prehistoric sight than a mob of emus loping along with their shivery grass skirts pulled up around their nuggety thighs.'

The birds can reach heights of two metres and weigh as much as 60 kilograms. Depending on the food availability they can range over distances greater than 500 kilometres, and reach speeds in excess of 60 kilometres per hour. They are strange birds. The males have a reputation for incubating beer stubbies or melons if eggs are smashed. They eat fruit, seeds, insects and flowers. One bird, however, was found to have the following stomach contents after it was shot: grass, general herbage, fruit, grain and coarse grit, a carpenter's steel pointed plumb-bob, two three-pin plastic electric wallplugs, one plug, one spring and three rubber doorstops. They have also been known to acquire a taste for paper, ice-cream cups, bottletops, keys, coins, brooches, cement powder and broken glass (which eventually emerges smooth-edged).

In an attempt to warn both kangaroos and emus that the fence is there old doggers and patrolmen often hang objects off the netting—everything from broken dog traps to old tins clattered and banged in the wind every few hundred metres as we drove.

Sandow wanted to show me Wynbring Rock. On 31 March 1875 Ernest Giles reached this spot. His arrival there was a miracle of Aboriginal navigation. A member of his party was an Aborigine, known to the Europeans as Jimmy. His proper name was Nanthona. 'In consequence,' wrote Giles, 'he was generally called Anthony, but he liked neither; he preferred Jimmy and asked me always to call him so.'

Jimmy had travelled to Wynbring as a child. Giles put his age at somewhere between fifty and seventy yet he found his way to the rockhole by remembering the stories he had been taught as a youngster:

> When at Youldeh [Ooldea] the old fellow had mentioned this spot, Wynbring, as the farthest water he knew to the eastwards, and now that we had arrived at it, he declared that beyond it there was nothing; it was the ultima thule of all his geographical ideas; he had never seen, heard or thought of anything beyond it. It was certainly a most agreeable little oasis, and an excellent spot for an explorer to come to in such a frightful region. Here were the three requisites that constitute an explorer's happiness—that is to say, wood, water and grass, there being splendid green feed and herbage on the few thousand acres of open ground around the rock. The old black guide had certainly brought us to this romantic and secluded little spot, with, I suppose I may say, unerring precision, albeit he wound about so much on the road, and made the distance far greater than it should have been. I was, however, struck with admiration at his having done so at all, and how he or any other human being, not having the advantages of science at his command to teach him, by the use of the heavenly bodies, how to find the position of any locality, could possibly return to the places we had visited in such a wilderness, especially as it was done by the recollection of spots which, to a white man, have no special features and

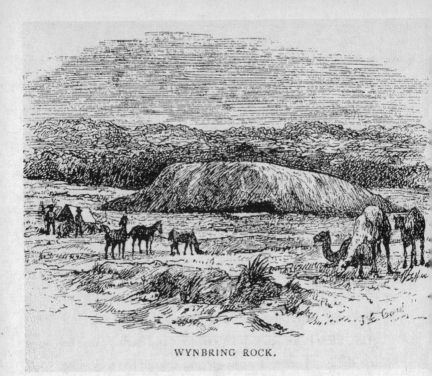

WYNBRING ROCK.

Wynbring as it appeared to Ernest Giles in 1875.

no guiding points, was really marvellous...In the course of a mile or so he would stop at a tree, and tell us that when a little boy he got a 'possum out of a hole which existed in it. At another place he said his mother was bitten by a wild dog, which she was digging out of a hole in the ground; and thus we came to Wynbring at last.

I too felt as though I had come to Wynbring the long way. It is an irony of the modern world that even with a global population of more than six billion people there are places that were once rich with humanity that are now deserted. Wynbring rockhole is one such spot. When Giles arrived, there were footprints everywhere and Jimmy disappeared briefly to return with five natives—an old man, three wives and a baby. All of them came up and embraced Giles warmly—the baby howled at being brought so close to a white man. The youngest wife was 'really very pretty, appeared enchantingly bashful, but what was her bashfulness compared to mine, when compelled for mere form's sake to enfold in my arms a beautiful and naked young woman?'

Giles wrote that the natives wanted to be given names. 'The young beauty I called Polly, the mother Mary, the baby Kitty, the oldest woman Judy, and to the old man I gave the name of Wynbring Tommy.'

The only footprints I could see around the rock belonged to stock. Sandow drove to Wynbring's summit, where the view was breathtaking. Stonemasons had built a rock wall around the base to increase the water catchment. The wall surrounded the entire outcrop.

With the help of dynamite, Europeans enlarged the waterhole to the size of an Olympic swimming pool. In places the rock walls are five metres deep and the water was green and putrid. Thick clouds of budgerigars wheeled overhead like holograms, changing colour with each shift in direction. There were also flocks of swallows and galahs. At the far end of the waterhole were a family of ducks, and thick as flies and not much bigger were swarms of zebra finches.

Wynbring today: a place that has changed little since the nineteenth century, except for the Telstra litter at its summit.

I pulled out Giles' journal and opened it at a sketch of Wynbring. Sandow and I were struck at the similarity 150 years later. Bill has been coming to Wynbring for three decades and never before knew of its connection to one of Australia's most successful explorers.

It was 11 am, 36 degrees Celsius and with no measurable humidity. Soon after we parked to have our morning orange in front of a sign warning us that we were about to cross into the Woomera Rocket Range and that any unauthorised entry was prohibited. It didn't stop a giant feral cat which came loping across a sand dune on the inside of the fence. When it saw us it bolted in the opposite direction.

Cats are destroying wildlife across the continent and were introduced into this region to reduce rabbit numbers. In 1900, rabbits were causing massive problems across South Australia and a consignment of 100 cats was released at Eucla on the southern edge of the Nullarbor. This story was like that of the old lady who swallowed the spider to catch the fly. The arrival of the cats was an ecological death sentence. By 1901 rabbits were in plague numbers at Ooldea. A few years later the rabbits were right through the Great Victoria Desert. The cats did nothing except contribute to a shameful number of native animal extinctions. Australia has the notorious honour of losing more small- to medium-sized mammals than any other country in the world.

'It's big but it looks half starved to me,' Sandow said, adding that he wished we had seen this feral cat in more open country so he could have shot it. Over the next month I would come to hate the sight of these intruders and feel intense frustration at the ill-informed colonists who first released them.

CHAPTER 4

DEATH FENCE

Bill Sandow knows where the Dog Fence in South Australia goes, but as we headed up into the country north of the railway line he told me that no one yet knows *exactly* where to put it on a map. For the first two years of the new millennium, using a global positioning system and a clipboard, Sandow took readings of the location of every bend in the fence between the Great Australian Bight and the New South Wales border. He sent thirty pages of co-ordinates to Canberra and soon hopes to complete his run with an accurate map in his glovebox. The location of the New South Wales fence is known because it traverses a line of longitude and then a line of latitude. But it may take years before each of the Queensland fence's many corners have been recorded with global positioning system equipment.

'Up to now the central mapping authority relied on where they thought it was,' Sandow explained. 'In a lot of places it's shown straight but it's actually got a lot of bends in it. No one had an exact geographic location of it. We see various maps and you know that they have just drawn the fence where they think it is.'

At first it seemed incredible that the fenceline had not been surveyed. As my journey progressed, however, I came across pastoralists who did not know their own property's boundaries, who could only tell me to within thousands of hectares how much land they own. Highlighting the emptiness and isolation of this stretch of fence is a tale told by its most famous and long-serving inspector. Len 'Doggy' Burton's tenure stretched from 1946 to 1964—it was under his reign that patrolmen upgraded from camels to cars. Burton once lost £25 on the Commonwealth Hill fence. When he returned three months later he found it caught in the netting.

By lunchtime it was 46.9 degrees outside and nearly 40 inside. Bill turned the airconditioning down, reasoning that it would be too much of a hot shock to clamber from the 'cool' of the cabin to the desert. In a little over an hour I had drunk two litres of juice. My other bottle was as warm as a tepid cup of tea. We were now running along the eastern boundary of one of the most infamous areas in Australia—Maralinga Prohibited Area. In the 1950s the British and Australian governments had tested nuclear bombs in the desert to our left. From 1953 to 1957 nine nuclear devices were detonated in the Great Victoria Desert—two at Emu and seven at Maralinga. They ranged in size from one kiloton to nearly twenty-seven. All of them were atmospheric tests and deposited radiation across the continent.

Len Beadell surveyed the Maralinga nuclear test sites as well as the Woomera Rocket Range. In his eyewitness account of the first nuclear test on mainland Australia in October 1953, Beadell wrote:

> The entire sky as it domed out and down past the distant horizon lit up in a blinding flash of fire and we felt the heat on our backs for a fleeting fraction of a second. No noise yet, apart from the screaming jets of the Canberra bomber as it made its run in. In just over a second we all whirled around to witness the end of the fireball and the boiling cauldron of deadly radioactive dust fighting for room to expand all at once…We had temporarily forgotten that there was supposed to be a noise and shockwave accompanying it, but we were soon reminded. At least there was a little warning—we saw a difference in the colour of the mulgas as they bent reflecting the sun at a different angle. This change in colour from normal dull green to almost light grey neared slowly at first as we were looking at it obliquely. Then when it got to within half a mile it seemed to race at us and we were nearly knocked over by its force.

The full extent of the blasts' impact on desert Aborigines will never be known as some families did not make their first contact with white society until the late 1980s. One of Australia's most famous indigenous leaders, Yami Lester, was blinded after a black radioactive cloud blew over his home. In his book *The Great Victoria Desert*, Mark Shephard writes of another terrible tragedy which became known as the 'Pom Pom' incident. It concerned Charlie and Edie Mulpuddie and their children Henry and Rosie. They were walking through the test range unaware of the harm they were doing themselves. 'On the morning of 14 May 1957 an astonished army officer found Charlie near the crater formed by the explosion at Marcoo seven months earlier.' The family had walked over at least 1.6 kilometres of contaminated land. Soon after, Edie's baby was stillborn. Her next child died at two of a brain tumour and Rosie miscarried in 1973. Scott Cane writes:

> How on earth could the Spinifex People comprehend, and in what manner could army patrol officers have possibly explained, that the land of the Spinifex People was about to be used as an atomic testing site? What did the Spinifex People know about the cold war, about Australia's place in the British Commonwealth of Nations, about atomic fission, radiation and cancer, or the half life of plutonium that would render 300 square kilometres of their country uninhabitable for the next 250,000 years?

Hundreds of servicemen were also affected by fallout from the blasts and debate about the adequacy of the clean-up undertaken in the worst affected areas continues today.

We drove past more and more carcasses, until almost every tree seemed to have animal remains underneath it, most of them camels. At first there was one every few kilometres, then every few hundred metres until we started to pass groups of up to fifty dead camels crowded under the shade of a single tree. The mummification process had frozen each corpse with an expression as though it had died screaming. Some had been shot while others died of thirst. A few weeks earlier, in January 2001, there had been forty-five successive days where the temperature in the region exceeded 40 degrees Celsius. Kangaroos, emus, birds and reptiles all perished in the heat. It was so hot that Sandow was ordered to stay in Adelaide. The camels are the most visible reminder of those hell-like weeks and nothing could have prepared me for the sight of 1000 corpses and at least as many kangaroo and emu remains. Along the Commonwealth Hill boundary alone 400 camels were shot and countless others succumbed to the heatwave.

The camels had headed south in search of water. When they hit the fence some broke through but most were too weak and died pressed up hard against the wire. The stench was incredible. Because of the amount of oil in a camel's

A camel graveyard along the Dog Fence near Commonwealth Hill Station.

hump, fetid fluid was still oozing out of their bodies a year after they had died. The Dog Fence Board dispatched a bulldozer in a futile attempt to clean up the carnage. The men had to sleep over 100 metres from their vehicles and earth-moving equipment to escape the smell. My nostrils were now full of the putrid stink. For hundreds of kilometres, whenever I got out of the car to eat or stretch while Sandow had a closer look at the fence, my hands absorbed death from the wind and smelt as though they had patted a dog that had rolled in something dead. No one knows exactly how many camels died in January 2001. A year later the skins had dried over the skeletons as taut as a drum. Hip bones stuck out through the leathery hides and were bleached so white that it was hard to look at them without sunglasses.

The person who gained the most from the mass death on the fence was an old Croatian dogger, Ted Grabovack. He severed hundreds of camel humps, laced them with strychnine and hung them on the fence to poison dingoes.

This was Ted's stretch of fence and Sandow told me how the old dogger loved to show off about the number of dingoes he had shot and trapped. He would hang the dead dogs off the top strand of wire and many such trophies were still there. In some places the whole dog was still hanging but mostly all that was left was what scavengers had not chewed away. In one place there were just two paws lashed onto the top strand of wire—the rest of the body had rotted or been dragged away.

A couple of months after the camels had swept through, seventy-five-year-old Ted died of a heart attack beside his car inside the fence. His body was found a few days later by another stationhand. 'Old Ted,' said Sandow, 'put the "t" in tough.'

Ted had a close association with the MacLachlan family. Hugh MacLachlan is one of the richest men in the country, the nation's biggest private landholder with an estate of sheep stations that covers five million hectares. He has, in fact, the largest sheep property in the world. 'It's the fence that allows us to run and breed merinos inside it,' MacLachlan told me. 'If the fence wasn't there the dogs would decimate us.'

Hugh had known old Ted most of his life and described him as 'diligent'—he always had his traps out, he always checked them and he knew where the dogs were. 'He was extraordinarily loyal to his employer but he was a bit of a law unto himself and quite hard to handle.'

Two hundred and sixty kilometres after leaving the railway line we finally made it to Mount Igy Corner. Sandow told me this is where the rocket scientists target their missiles and there is a sixty-kilometre exclusion zone next to where we were standing. We stood on the outside of the corner but inside, over the wire and funnelled into the dead end, were the bones of hundreds of emus and kangaroos. Corners in the Dog Fence, I was quickly discovering, had a huge impact on wildlife—kangaroos and emus followed the wire until they were corralled into small areas without food and water.

Fifteen kilometres further on Sandow suddenly exclaimed, 'Oi, who the devil is this?' He pulled over towards a leathery-looking guy sitting in a chair beside his vehicle, smoking, drinking a beer and reading a Clive Cussler novel. It was Dean Jaensch, the patrolman for the Commonwealth Hill boundary. He was wearing shorts, boots and a threadbare blue T-shirt. Sandow had a dig at him for looking so relaxed when there were two hours of daylight left. Jaensch didn't seem to find the joke funny. He was immersed in his book, the cover of which was of big snow-clad mountains. Sandow introduced me and told Jaensch that I was writing a book on the fence. 'I'm happy for ya,' he said, not sounding happy at all.

Jaensch's camp looked familiar—it was almost exactly the same layout as Sandow's and I later learnt that the two men had been stationhands together thirty years ago at Commonwealth Hill. Jaensch's bed, which was an old steel-framed, fold-up cot, was situated with the head at the driver's side door. There was a worn and filthy piece of canvas laid out on the desert as a mat near the head of the bed. Everything was very neat and organised, as if he were expecting visitors. A big fire was set and he had a steel barbecue with a windbreak ready to cook his dinner.

Before he had stopped for the day Jaensch had shot three camels a kilometre inside the fence and fixed up a huge hole the beasts had made when they pushed through the netting. Two of the camels had dropped instantly, the third had run off bellowing and squirting a trail of blood. 'He'll die out there somewhere, the cunt,' Jaensch said, then drew on his cigarette and sipped his beer. Dingo numbers had been a bit down and in the last year Jaensch said he had only shot four. After an awkward minute of idle talk about the fence and promises to deliver more netting and dog traps it was clear that Jaensch wanted to get back to his book. Sandow, too, was keen to move on. Grey thunder clouds with swirling charcoal undersides had built up above us. At this point along the fence, rain would be a major setback that could stop us getting to Coober Pedy the next day. We said our farewells and were on our way.

Half an hour later we set up our own camp in the swale between two bright red sand dunes, east of the Garfield gate. It was Valentines Day and I asked Bill if I could make a quick call to my wife on his satellite phone. While we ate dinner— lamb chops and baked potatoes—we talked again about Giles' journey. When I told Sandow about the difficulties Giles had navigating through the desert—how he was reliant on the stars for his location and the boiling point of water to determine his altitude—Bill walked over to his glovebox and pulled out his global positioning system. It was not much bigger than a packet of cigarettes and soon we had our exact location, accurate to a few metres. I was 1734 kilometres from my home in Sydney and at a height of 176 metres. Sandow gave me the GPS and told me to walk towards Sydney. The reading said that I was travelling at three kilometres per hour but after another twenty metres I hit the fence and turned back.

We had also settled into an evening routine of pulling out my bird and reptile books and working out together what we had seen during the day. Whether it was the pre-storm humidity or just bad luck, Sandow's light was attracting a prehistoric jungle's worth of invertebrates around our camp. Of greatest concern to me, considering that I was sleeping in the open on the ground, were two enormous scorpions—both at least twelve centimetres long, with big nippers and tail stingers. I followed one with my torch as it manoeuvred over and under twigs and leaves, like a creature from a science-fiction movie. Sandow reassured me with a chortle that it wasn't deadly.

As I lay on my mat I could see the Aboriginal constellation of the emu. It sits below the Southern Cross and is made up of an immense emptiness—dark bands of nebulae silhouetted against the glow of the Milky Way, and shaped exactly like the neck and head of one of the birds I had followed that day along the fence. It is only visible far away from the glow of major cities and towns. I could see lightning and then felt a few drops of rain. Fearing a storm and also concerned about the scorpions I decided, for the first time, to put up my tent. By the time I was inside a hot strong wind was blowing which ripped the pegs straight out of the ground. I secured them a second time, climbed back in and spent the night sleeping on a film of sweat between myself and the ground mat.

Sandow was keen to get moving before the sun was up. Between us and Coober Pedy was a series of salt lakes that the fence went straight across, and after rain they become impassable. 'When this country gets wet it's like a big pot of bloody custard,' Sandow said. 'When she's dry she's like cement.'

We crossed the salt lakes and I imagined the surface of Mars. The dawn light was also weird. The only thing that indicated I was still on Earth was the Dog Fence.

The turnoff to Emu Junction was at the place where Sandow woke up in the middle of the night with the dingo sniffing in his ear. On the morning of his close encounter Bill packed up his camp, climbed in his four-wheel-drive and slowly followed the tracks of the dog. After six kilometres he came across the dingo and shot him.

As we travelled we discovered two sets of fresh tracks in the red sand. Bill slowed down but after a few kilometres the tracks headed into the scrub. There are so few corners in the South Australian fence that a turn is simply named after the nearest station. Even if the station is hundreds of thousands of hectares in size, confusion is almost impossible. Any change of direction that I could see on my map would be something I began to anticipate hours before a bend arrived.

At Mabel Creek Corner there was another scene of devastation—the previous year hundreds of emus got stuck and died there, unable to pass through the Dog Fence. Sandow also told me that for years some black lingerie had been left hanging on the gate—a pair of lacy undies and a bra. 'You would get to it after two weeks in the scrub and sit and stare and wonder where she was.'

Travellers used to be able to rely on water pumped by windmills from bores along this stretch. At Mabel Creek there is water in the bottom of the well but the windmill no longer works. Nobody is there to look after the equipment and sometimes even the stock. When Sandow last did the run past the station he had to let cattle out of one paddock into another because they were dying of thirst. Windmills require constant attention—their pipes crack when water freezes inside them during the winter. Sometimes 'wind droughts' mean it might not blow for weeks on end and the windmills become useless. Mostly, however, the Great Victoria Desert was one of the windiest places that I had ever experienced. At first I could not understand how Sandow could dislike the wind as much as he did, but a few hours from Coober Pedy I changed my mind. At night it roared, malicious, unending, as though you were its specific target.

By the time of our morning orange we were at the north-ernmost point of the fence in South Australia. The distinctive sand dunes and mulga were giving way to great plains of stones and dust that shimmered with mirages. Heading towards one windmill, which looked only a short distance away, Sandow said, 'See how close that looks? It's a mirage.' Sure enough we drove at least five kilometres before we reached it.

We crossed the central Australian railway and an hour later reached the Stuart Highway. We were now in a completely different world. The geology was different, the horizon was different, the vegetation was different and the Dog Fence looked frail enough for a child to push it over. Also, it was hard to imagine what it was doing there. This was an area so denuded of life that it was chosen for the filming of the Hollywood blockbuster, *Red Planet*.

In the film there is a scene where the actor Val Kilmer runs out of oxygen in his spacesuit and lifts his visor, certain he is to die. Instead he discovers that the Martian air has become breathable. The first time I stepped out of the air-conditioned car and filled my lungs with heated Coober Pedy oxygen, it felt as though *I* couldn't breathe.

The Coober Pedy patrolman, Jeff Boland, has what some would describe as a thankless job. Fenceposts in his section can only be put into the ground with a rock auger because the soil is only a few centimetres deep. 'There's no point waiting for it to soften with rain,' Sandow said, 'because you might be waiting for years.'

The flipside of this is that once a post is in place it will be there until the end of time. 'If you use local trees the wood lasts forever, but even if you bring in a post from just one hundred kilometres away they rot in no time. The meshing stands forever out here because there's nothing to rust it.'

In this landscape I noticed another strange optical illusion. If I looked at the posts on the fence for a few minutes and then glanced up to the sky, it seemed as though the clouds were being sucked down towards the horizon. I mentioned this to Sandow and he said that he often goes to sleep with the Dog Fence passing like a movie on the inside of his eyelids.

Sandow wanted to show me a landscape utterly devoid of vegetation, but when we got to the Moon Plain near Coober Pedy he was bitterly disappointed. 'The moonscape's got bloody grass on it!' A good rain the year before had given the soil a five o'clock shadow. Finches played around the fence, flying straight through its netting as if it wasn't even there. They timed their wing flaps for the precise moment they passed through the wire, wheeling from one side to the other as though they were ghosts moving through a wall. Bigger birds stuck in the wire had become mummified. That evening was to be the last that Sandow and I were to spend together and we opted to camp on the Dog Fence where it crosses the road to Oodnadatta. After dark we could see the lights of Coober Pedy which looked like stars that had come down to rest in the Breakaways.

It was not until we reached Coober Pedy that I felt the characters I had met in Ceduna were really left behind. No matter who you are in Ceduna, there's a good chance that beyond Mount Igy Corner you are unknown. Dropping the name of someone I had met along the fence usually had currency for about 500 kilometres and then I would cross some invisible line beyond which the name was unfamiliar. The fence is like a guitar string that sings the tune of the area it passes through.

That night Sandow helped me make arrangements for the rest of my journey along the South Australian fence. We contacted landholders right through to the New South Wales border to let them know I was on my way. He offered a few last words of wisdom about driving over sand dunes and suggested I buy some water containers.

Just before Bill went to bed he told me that when we had left Ceduna he had been worried I would not enjoy the trip, that I would find nothing to write about or would be afraid of the isolation. He once had a passenger who became irrational and terrified when a storm hit, stranding them for a few days. I told him I wished he was coming for the rest of my journey but he assured me the book would be better for my being on my own.

CHAPTER 5

THE MOON PLAIN

Sandow checked over my hired four-wheel-drive as if he were a father helping his son buy his first car. As soon as he drove off, I headed for the laundromat. Within ten minutes I was joined by a group of tourists. The backpackers were Swedish and were trying to scrape together enough change to do two loads of washing. Soon after, a pair of bleary-eyed miners came in drinking beer even though it wasn't yet 9 am. The miners were from out of town and said they only got into Coober once or twice a fortnight. 'Have you found many opals?' I asked cheerfully.

The younger of the pair raised his VB in its stubby holder and swept it in an arc. 'D'ya think I'd fuckin' be here if I had?' His teeth were rotten, his beard was matted with dust and when I shook his hand it was so callused and rough that it felt more like hide.

The cycle was finished and I wanted to get back to the fence even though my clothes were wet. There was a fifty-kilometre section between the Stuart Highway and Coober Pedy that Sandow and I had missed. It meant backtracking, but I was determined to travel every millimetre of the structure. Half an hour later I stopped at a sign—the bonnet of an old Holden decorated with an exaggerated legend of the Dog Fence. It is one of the few places where the existence of the fence is touted so prominently.

> You're crossing…THE DOG FENCE. This 5,600 km fence runs from Surfers Paradise, Qld, to the Bight near WA. Dingoes are found to the north—in cattle country. Protected sheep country to the south.

The bonnet is an *objet d'outback*, the perfect prop for silver nomads and backpackers to pose in front of to prove that they have seen the fence.

I drove for ten kilometres along the fence before I felt far enough from Coober Pedy to hang my washing. Within twenty minutes my clothes were dried to the texture of cardboard. I was on my own and I was euphoric. I hadn't showered in nearly a week but my clothes were now clean and dry and I had my own vehicle to take me to New South Wales and Queensland. I had never driven a four-wheel-drive before and I was about to tackle the most rugged and isolated track in Australia. I had food and water, my sleeping bag, ground mat, a borrowed tarpaulin, a plate, knife, fork, spoon, cup and a case of beer. My mobile phone didn't work and at that

Coober Pedy clothesline. The hills in the background are called breakaways.

moment no one knew exactly where I was.

I folded my clothes and organised my stuff. Driving this section would bring me back to the Stuart Highway in a loop around to Coober. I would see what the car could do and find out if there was anything I needed.

Sandow had warned me that there was a washed-out creek ahead that had challenged even *his* four-wheel-drive skills. He told me to find a way around it. I soon discovered what he meant. A sedan was bogged in the middle of the track and my heart started to race as I thought of wild Coober locals. There was no one around. Inside the car were dirty clothes and two jerry cans on the back seat. With a few millimetres to spare I drove around only to discover that an erosion gully had eaten away a third of the track. To the left of the passenger-side wheel was a metre-deep drop, exactly where the edge of my wheel would have to pass if I was to go any further. I put the car into four-wheel-drive, then slowly nudged forward. The car sloped down on a forty-five-degree angle, taking me dangerously close to the crack. How humiliating would it be to get stuck one hour into my freedom? I could feel the ground giving way on the driver's side. I put my foot on the accelerator and surged out of the creek bed and back onto the plain.

Soon afterwards I stopped, climbed over the Dog Fence and walked towards one of the breakaways in the distance. In other states similar hills are called jump-ups. Basically they are eroded outliers of the ranges that once existed around Coober Pedy. Scree covered the peaks' flanks and in both directions I could see the Dog Fence snaking away over the horizon. To my left was the Great Australian Bight and thousands of dead camels. Dean Jaensch would have finished his Cussler novel by now, Chris Richards was lancing camel abscesses and Ceduna was still stewing in its soup of racial disquiet.

At that moment on top of the breakaway I was as close

to the heart of the Australian continent as the fence travels. A few days earlier, back in the Great Victoria Desert, I had in a heat-induced torpor watched ants patrolling the ground beneath my feet. Now I reflected how, except for invertebrates and other hardy desert-adapted wildlife, Australia resembles a giant centrifuge which spins people away from its centre to its shoreline. From the summit I could see how antlike humanity is in the vast space of a desert wilderness. My car was a white speck far below and the Dog Fence looked like the thread of a cobweb. I was small and I was alone, the closest human was in Coober Pedy and if something went wrong and I was unable to move it would be up to a fortnight before the patrolman next came along this way. The ants, however, would find me within seconds.

It was only two hours since I had left the laundromat but already I was having noisy internal conversations. It was as if for the first time in my life I could hear myself thinking. In the city I feel as though I am swept along in a current of timetables, appointments, deadlines and responsibilities. Out by the fence I felt the social equivalent of weightlessness.

To my right was another slab of the continent that is rarely visited. Between myself and the end of the South Australian fence—a distance of over 1000 kilometres—was one major settlement, Roxby Downs, and two minor outposts, Marree and Arkaroola. Except for the people who lived and worked near the fence and whom I had arranged to meet,

I did not expect to see another soul.

After another two hours of driving I headed back into Coober Pedy. The conical rubble piles left by the opal miners filled the landscape. The diggings looked frantic—there was none of the total destruction that follows one big mine, yet somehow the thousands of little ones I could see seemed far worse. The spoil heaps stretched over the horizon, having accumulated without consideration of their proximity to town or their aesthetic effect. Coober Pedy is at heart about turning the ground inside out until it has given up the last of its jewels. When I visited the supermarket the noticeboard was layered with photocopied, computer-printed and hand-written sheets advertising secondhand noodlers, blowers and tunnellers for sale.

I went in search of a shower and found one associated with an underground shop called the Opal Cave. Outside, in the carpark, was a building-sized metal spaceship that must have been left by some film crew, but there was no explanation of the intergalactic craft. My shower took two and a half minutes and I wasn't sure whether I felt one or two million dollars better. It was the first time in a week that I had smelt nice.

Sharon and Wayne Rankin own the Twins sheep station, my next stop down the Dog Fence, and I called them from a Coober Pedy payphone, hotter than the insides of a slow combustion wood oven. The Dog Fence between Coober Pedy and Roxby Downs is the most remote in the state. I had to travel through the Woomera Prohibited Area. I had permission to do so from the pastoralists and the Dog Fence Board but not from the federal government. Sometimes, as Australian journalist Peter Smark used to say, *one must assume permission.*

Sandow had advised me to go to the Rankins via the highway and I knew he would be annoyed to learn that I was planning to drive into the desert by myself. Wayne Rankin, however, assured me that unless I was stupid I would be fine. When I am stressed I get big rosy cheeks, and by the time Rankin had given me directions to his homestead, telling me to look out for a pointy hill, I was glowing.

'Don't worry,' he said. 'You turn off the fence at the whistling willy gate. You won't be able to miss it.' I thanked him and hung up. What the hell was a whistling willy gate?

I had one last thing to do before I left Coober. I have never played golf before, but there they have the strangest course on Earth and that night I was invited for a barbecue followed by a night game. The clubhouse of the Coober Pedy Opal Fields Golf Club is on the summit of what looks like a slag heap, with a view over the eighteen-hole course and back towards the town. On arrival I was greeted with the offer of a beer by club captain Stuart Jackson and the comment, 'I would like to say it's one of the top ten desert courses in the world, but it's not. It's on a list somewhere for the most unusual course.'

Golf in Coober Pedy is mostly a winter game. Apart

from playing at dawn and dusk it is close to impossible to have a round in mid-February. There are about eighty members of the club, the fairways are desert and the greens are called scrapes. 'Our scrapes are just oil and sand mixed together so they don't blow away in a willy willy,' Jackson informed me. Before dinner a hole-in-one competition was held with the prize of a free ticket to the barbecue. I had decided to wait until the night golf proper was under way so I could hit my first golf ball under the cover of darkness. But soon I realised that everyone was there simply to have fun. At Coober Pedy every golfer can be a dusty Tiger Woods. Surrounded by such a big group of happy people, I could understand why this could be a good place to live.

At 9 pm we headed down the hill in little drunken groups to tee off. The round was to be played on Ambrose rules, which means that you play on from the ball hit the furthest by a member of your team. With the sky totally black and awash with the Milky Way and the desert all around, I had an inkling of what Apollo astronaut Al Shepard experienced when he belted a golf ball across the lunar plains.

Each team carried a little square of fake grass to put under their balls, which at night become fluorescent green and sail across the sky like meteorites. A 'booze bus' drove around the course from one team to the other distributing beer. By 11 pm our team had only completed two holes. At the pace we were moving the game was going to last until dawn. After dozens of attempts I finally hit one cracking shot which made me appreciate why two of my best friends are addicted to golf. Exhausted, I excused myself and drove back to the fence to sleep in the same little sand hollow Sandow and I had camped in the night before. I woke to a spectacular sunrise. A sheet of grey blanketed the sky, except for a tiny slice just above the horizon. When the sun appeared through this crack it caught the whole underbelly of the clouds and lit them with infinite variations of orange, pink, purple and red.

I was on the southern boundary of the world's biggest cattle station, Anna Creek, which is 23,890 square kilometres. For the first few hours of driving the ground looked as if somebody had mulched it with smashed bottles—it is in fact gypsum, tens of thousands of hectares of it. In the age of the dinosaurs this landscape was near the South Pole. Australia was part of the super-continent Gondwana, and an ocean called the Eromanga Sea covered all of this area. Icebergs would have floated above the dry sea floor that I was now standing on. These blocks of ice contained rubble and boulders which settled to the sea floor when the bergs melted.

Plesiosaurs and ichthyosaurs hunted in this ocean, the top-order predators in the polar seas. It is possible to walk around the Moon Plain east of Coober Pedy and discover the full fossilised skeleton of one of these reptiles. And in 2001, less than fifty metres from the Dog Fence, palaeontologists from the South Australian Museum did exactly that.

For the first time since I had left Ceduna it was cool. At midday more breakaway country began to appear—separated by a mirage from the horizon. A green tinge on these mountains indicates mega-rich deposits of organic material left as the Cretaceous marine ecosystem dried up. If this region had been capped by clay it may have become one of the world's great gas deposits; instead it is a barely explored fossil resource which promises decades of discoveries before all its secrets have been extracted.

I came to a pointy hill standing alone which looked like the mountain Rankin had described, but it was inside the fence. I climbed over the netting and walked towards it. Normally when a range crumbles its remains are carried far away, but here pieces simply fell as if the rock were being sculpted and the discarded chips left on the floor of a studio. There were a billion years of stone chips scattered within a few hundred metres of the hill, which made walking treacherous. From its summit I could see a track heading north into Anna Creek Station, the Dog Fence and, on another distant summit, what looked like a survey marker. The landscape around me was stripped to its bare essentials. On the very highest point was a fist-sized rock and on top of that was a kangaroo's paw, complete with a knuckle's worth of skin. I thought of my nine-year-old son Angus because a month earlier he had found the velociraptor-like fighting claw of a male eastern grey kangaroo and made a necklace out of it. I chose to leave *this* claw where it was. On top of that hill I felt as lonely as a ghost.

At first glance the hill had seemed devoid of life. On my way down, though, I scared a falcon and then a wasp intimidated me into wild arm-waving by swooping at my face. I now saw that the hill was teeming with life—there were wildflowers, trees so stunted they could have been bonsais, the ever-present legions of ants. A dragon lizard fled under a stone, I uncovered a spider nest, and wallaby dung lay sprinkled on the ground like little chocolate Easter eggs.

I climbed back over the fence, got into my car and after a few kilometres was in another ecosystem altogether. The empty Moon Plain was behind me and I was travelling through a small rugged range, followed by fields of gibber. Soon after a gate appeared, held up with posts the like of which I had never seen before. They stood taller than me, had the circumference of a strong man's arm with slits down their side. As soon as I saw it I knew that what was in front of me must be a whistling willy gate. To ensure this was my turnoff to the Twins Station I decided to follow the fence for a few more kilometres. I came to yet another whistling willy post gate and then a third. The country was now rough and intimidating, littered with stones that made my vehicle slide on the Dog Fence track. In other places the layer of gibber was gone, exposing sand.

Time was on my side as I had arranged to arrive at the

Rankins' station around 6 pm. I decided to drive for one more hour and then turn back if I hadn't found another whistling willy gate. Rankin had told me to turn off at the whistling willy—had I reached it? Which was the right one?

The country became even rougher and I feared that I would soon damage my car if I kept going. I came to a rise that allowed me to see at least ten kilometres towards the horizon. There was no break in the gibber-covered mountains and I could not see any other gates through my binoculars. I turned the car around and in doing so staked one of my tyres on a saltbush, flattening it within seconds. The clouds had gone and it was now baking hot. The thermometer inside the car read 40 degrees. By the time I had changed the tyre I was flustered and worried—which gate would take me to my destination? Keen to be back with people and off the fence, I decided that I would go through the first one I came back to.

I opened the gate in the Dog Fence and drove away from the only sure thing I knew at that moment. Once inside I began looking for the next landmark—a fork in the road. It never came and I started to panic. In my hurry to find something I could identify, I drove over a gutter across the track that smashed my chassis so hard I thought I must have snapped something. All around me were broken-down fences that had marked previous lines in the sand against feral pests.

For the second time that day I thought about my children—this time my seven-year-old son, Finn. When I first bought some land on the east coast I put a caravan on it. At the time Finn was three and a city boy who had spent all his life in flats in Sydney. He refused to leave the van and every now and then I saw his terrified face pushing aside the curtains to look outside at all the space. For the first time I truly understood how he had felt.

I decided to head due west, knowing that I would at least eventually hit the Stuart Highway. After an hour I came to a gate with a well-used dusty track heading south. I put my foot down and within seconds the car was submerged in powdery bulldust, which ran down every window like a liquid. After the windscreen cleared, a few hundred metres ahead I could see a big drilling rig operated by two guys who looked as if they had walked off the set of *Mad Max*. The mud-soaked boss directed me back the way I had come and then through a different gate which would lead me to the homestead. On the way I passed another mining camp where a young, filthy man confirmed I was on the right track to the Rankins. Closer still a convoy of mining trucks hurtled past and I would later learn that Minotaur Mining were exploring for gold and copper.

Just on 6 pm I pulled into the Twins homestead. Sheep mustering was in full swing and the entire shearing crew was in the yards near the house. Getting to the station without having to be rescued seemed like a minor miracle to me and I wanted to make a dignified entrance. What I hadn't expected was my first meeting with a cocky gate. I had no idea that such a complicated method of getting through a fence had ever been invented. All eight men mustering had stopped work to watch my arrival. I got out of the car and sauntered over to the gate to open it. I walked to one end and it defied my fiddling. The same at the other end. I decided to cut my losses and climb over. I walked up to the mustering yards where Wayne Rankin came over and took my hand in a crushing clasp. He told me to bring the vehicle through the gate and go over to the homestead. He would join me in fifteen minutes. 'Sorry to seem like an idiot,' I said, 'but how do you open the gate?'

'Don't worry,' he reassured me, 'there's another one over there, you should be able to get through that.'

Rankin went back to his mustering while I moved the car and made my way to the main house. Pastoralists lead lives very different from those of most Australians. The homestead for each property is more like a small village, with many families living together. The Twins Station was busy with mustering and shearing and at these times the kitchen is a hub of activity: cooking, smoking, eating, talking, child-minding, planning and socialising. Sharon Rankin took my hand in a grip almost as fierce as her husband's and introduced herself. She seemed equal parts intimidating and nervous and wanted to know at once what I was doing along the fence. Like her husband she had a reputation for being tough and fair, and was well-respected. She had short brown hair, was wearing jeans and boots, and gave the impression of wielding her share of power in the Rankin marriage. It was the first home I had entered along the fence and I was taken aback by the Rankins' hospitality and friendliness.

In 1950 a young constable, Clair Bottroff, wrote his parents a letter extolling the hospitality of Wayne's parents when he passed through on his way to Coober Pedy. Discovering his letter a few days later made me feel as though I had been trapped in a time warp:

> Mrs Rankin, the owner's wife, took us inside red with dust and oozing with perspiration as we were. I have become an ardent tea drinker since being up here, & have tasted some nice brews, but the 3 cups that Mrs Rankin gave me were the best to date.

I was also surprised to learn that the Rankins are neighbours with Commonwealth Hill Station—where I had bumped into Dean Jaensch, hundreds of kilometres ago and several days earlier. My brain was still coming to terms with the change of scale from suburban Sydney to central Australia.

Sharon had been a boundary rider along the Dog Fence for fifteen years, only giving up the job about four years ago. 'I would leave on a Friday night after school of the air and camp Friday and Saturday night,' she told me. 'Even when the children were babies we would put them in a bassinette and off we would go.' Once she was attaching netting when the gun put a nail through her finger and into the post. Her car was close by but she could not quite reach either her two-way radio or her wire cutters. She tried to pull her hands free. A stationhand and Sharon's two children had set up camp near a creek more than a kilometre away and although they were visible she could not get their attention by either waving or shouting. Eventually her daughter Emma observed, 'Mum seems to have been in the same place for a long time.'

After a brief chat Sharon invited me to put anything I needed cold into the fridge, a separate building where months of supplies are stored. The kitchen table was big enough and worn enough to have done a Viking feasting hall proud. On the stove was a kettle the size of my biggest pot at home. In the next few weeks I would learn that this item is one of the most important possessions of every property along the Dog Fence. All day it sits simmering so that a brew can be made at any time. Several loaves of bread sat beside the stove, next to an open tub of margarine and Vegemite.

Sharon also offered me a shower, welcome words considering I was coated in enough bulldust to make me look like a concreter. By the time I reappeared Wayne was sitting on a stool, drinking a beer and enjoying the last half-hour of dusk. He quickly finished two cans and then offered to take me on his 'rocket tour'.

CHAPTER 6

ROCKETS IN LAMB LAND

I joined the navy when I was seventeen years old and within weeks of signing up I found myself on a guided missile frigate off the south coast of New South Wales with a group of other young recruits to watch the launch of a million-dollar rocket. We were allowed to stand on the deck as the weapon took off from the ship with a roar. Within a second all that was left of the missile was its vapour trail, which formed a strip of cloud across a brilliant blue sky. Its target was an object towed by an unmanned supersonic aircraft called *Jindivik*. Though I did not know it on that sunny, memorable day at sea, both the missile and the target were created and tested in the desert half a continent away at the Woomera Rocket Range.

It is one of the strangest facts in Australian history that an area the size of England sits in the centre of the nation, off limits to all but authorised visitors (and sheep farmers), where rockets and weapons from around the world have been tested

The centrepiece of Wayne Rankin's rocket tour—something to look out on while you take a shower.

for nearly half a century. Wayne Rankin's entire property is within the rocket range and all his life he has collected as many of the fired missiles that have landed nearby as he has been able to find. The missile remains don't belong to him but Wayne Rankin has the look of a man who could easily stare down a rocket scientist. Years ago many municipal parks in Australia had a rusty steel-pipe rocket mounted onto concrete for children to climb inside and spin a wobbly steering wheel. Rankin owns the real thing. The first stop on his backyard rocket tour is a two-metre-square concrete slab. On top of it is a rocket, whose nose cone has been peeled back like banana skin from the force of the impact as it slammed into a sand dune not far from the homestead. 'I don't know what it is, but it had something to do with supernovas,' he said. I was speechless to see such a hi-tech piece of Australian space age history being accorded the status of a garden gnome. The other missiles he produced from his shed were decades old but of a special vintage and the nose cones were still in perfect condition.

The next stop was a white-domed observatory, which once would have housed a large telescope. It was retrieved from the rocket range one night after a few beers. 'I got it for a cubby for my daughter,' Rankin explained totally po-faced.

Sandow had told me that when he was a young stationhand at Commonwealth Hill in the 1970s he and the other staff would sit in bomb shelters and watch rockets fly overhead at night as entertainment—the ultimate cold-war fireworks display. These shelters are now over forty-five years old. The inside of the Rankin shelter had the atmosphere of a wine cellar, cool and dry, protected by thousands of sandbags piled on top of a semicircular steel frame and then covered with earth and grass. Because the shelter is oriented east–west, beautiful hay-coloured sunlight streamed in through the western end. At a princely cost of £127,000, forty-eight shelters were built to protect around 100 pastoralists, their families, staff and local Aborigines.

For the first decade after their construction the shelters were segregated. This fact is still a source of embarrassment for some of the pastoralists. Every bomb shelter and homestead in the firing line was also equipped with a telephone—a massive technological leap for some of Australia's most remote citizens. Thirteen thousand trials, mostly military, have been conducted on the range. Up until the 1980s more than 4000 rockets were launched and 3500 bombs dropped, ninety high altitude parachute drops made and six tests of ejector seats. There were 500 upper-atmosphere research flights, including 200 Skylark rockets, which once aloft 'had no more guidance than a Guy Fawkes rocket'.

Most ordinary people would have refused to tolerate such a bizarre combination of the space age and the cold war invading their skies. In Peter Morton's history of Woomera, *Fire across the Desert*, he writes that the bomb shelters grew out of the tension between guaranteeing safety, keeping costs down and reassuring powerful pastoral families without interrupting the testing. Originally there was a plan to have a thirty-kilometre exclusion zone around each homestead but it was thought that too many launches would have to be aborted. Another proposal was that World War II-style trenches should be constructed, into which bomb-weary sheep farmers would be asked to cower—sometimes for hours on a daily basis. The shelters that survive today are a compromise designed to protect occupants from flying debris or a nearby blast. They are not made to protect occupants from a direct hit. Before a rocket launch the graziers would get three warnings by telephone from the test headquarters at the 'rangehead'—the final take-cover was fifteen minutes before blast-off.

The risk was real but probably infinitesimal. For the famous Black Knight series of tests, which began in 1958 and concluded in 1965, it was estimated that 80 per cent of the rockets would fall in a predicted impact area. Half of the remaining flights could be aborted and cut down early, still close to the launch site. This still left 10 per cent, however, soaring unpredictably across the desert sky. 'The only report of casualties in more than thirty years came from the Manners Creek Station in the Northern Territory,' writes Morton. 'In 1967, during the trials of the large satellite launcher rocket *Europa I*, a stockman claimed to have found the corpses of three cows on the property surrounded by metal wreckage. One of the cows was graphically described as having been thrown into a tree by the blast.' The Commonwealth government accepted responsibility and paid compensation for the dead stock.

'It is hard to say how much the shelters were used,' Morton continues:

> At first some…of the residents dutifully retreated into them. Others quickly got transformed into games rooms or hay stores…When Black Knight began to be launched

in the hours of darkness, watching the fiery trails slashed across the velvet sky by the re-entry head as it plummeted to Earth became a popular activity all over the outback. By this time practically no one was bothering to take cover.

Mrs Flo Crombie, who once ran Mount Eba Station and was regarded as one of the range's toughest characters, told range superintendent Dick Durance:

They sent us a notice. Black Knight was going up. First it was seventy-two hours, then twenty-four hours, and at last they told us to take cover in the shelter. 'Course, we weren't in it. In fact the whole household was standing on top of it to get a good look. The rocket went up in the dark but it produced flashes every few seconds so you could see it climbing. It went up and up and everyone was enjoying the show. Then it turned over and began to come down. All the stockhands thought it was falling on them, and it did fall only a few miles away. I turned round to speak to the men and there wasn't a bastard there, Dick, not one bastard, and I was washing under-pants for a week after!

By the early sixties some properties were ordered to take cover every day and the pastoralists started to work right through the firings. Some took their phones off the hook and others refused to take calls after 11 pm.

'You just get used to it,' Wayne told me. 'And if one landed on you it would be instant death. It's part of our life, we live in this area and this area is a rocket range. We just have to change our lives a little bit.'

The rockets and the miners I had seen earlier in the afternoon were reminders of the nature of the tenure that the Rankin family have over their pastoral lease. They do not own the land, they share it.

At that we joined the crowd of shearers, stationhands, children and dogs. The talk began with the price of sheep, which was currently at an exciting high. Sheep are very important to Wayne and to everybody there—they provide food, a lifestyle, income and a constant topic for discussion. Wayne's second favourite subject that evening was how different life is today from when he was a kid. 'There used to be twenty people living here. Now you can't even get enough people for a game of cricket.'

'What on earth is a whistling willy gate?' I asked Wayne. He explained that the slitted poles were used to string the telephone lines around the rocket range. Many local pastoralists recycled them as fenceposts only to discover that in the strong desert winds they whistled so loudly that sometimes the noise was unbearable. My next question was about the other type of gate which had foiled my entrance. 'How is anyone expected to open it?' Rankin laughed loudly and said he was impressed I admitted feeling like a goose and promised

The curse of the outback is the cocky gate. This one is as user-friendly as they get.

to show me how to unlatch the cocky gate in the morning. I decided then that it was best to be candid when I didn't have a clue about what was going on.

Breakfast was dinner from the night before soaked in a delicious gravy, with sugary strong tea. Just after dawn I was planning to head down to Mount Eba Station and then on to Billa Kalina where I was meeting boundary rider Keith Beelitz for his three-day run from the Mount Eba Corner to Roxby

Downs. I asked Wayne, as a grazier, what he thought of the Dog Fence. Without it, he told me, he could not survive. He only sees the structure a few times a year in spite of the fact that it runs for eighty-odd kilometres along his boundary. 'I have seen dingoes living with sheep for three or four months without killing one,' Rankin said, looking as crisp as a fresh apple in spite of the beers the night before, which had left me decidedly crusty. 'We could see the tracks among the sheep and when we finally saw him we shot him.'

Rankin's point is that not all dogs are sheep killers. 'If they're starving they'll try and kill sheep and if there's lots of pups around they'll chase sheep for fun. The dingo pup is exactly the same as your sheep dog. Even in a chihuahua the instinct to kill is there.'

A golden rule at the Twins is that if you cannot be certain of hitting a dingo when you shoot it then leave it. 'Otherwise they get gun-shy,' Sharon told me. Last year she saw a dingo inside the fence and chased it across the paddock in her four-wheel-drive, eventually tiring it out before running it over. Dingo numbers have been low in recent years and only five were shot the previous year by station staff.

As I was about to walk out the door Sharon asked if I had seen some wire down on the creek near the fence. I had but registered it as litter that had washed into a tree during a flood. 'That wire in the tree was Bill Stretton's. He used it as a receiver for his radio.'

Wayne had known Bill Stretton throughout his childhood, and to him the old patrolman was a true frontiersman. A tough, short, independent character, he was 'a fiery red-haired man with a big red beard', Rankin remembered. 'I only ever called him Mr Stretton. He was a very prompt, very precise man.' Stretton gained renown for, among other things, righting his Land Rover with a fence strainer after he rolled it, and for winning a bottle of whisky in a bet after carrying a rainwater tank on his back.

Rankin showed me how to open a cocky gate but I would be well into Queensland before I could be sure of remembering the procedure. They work on the principle that an iron bar is twisted through loose wire and then used as a lever to pull the entire contraption taut.

An hour down the road was Mount Eba Station, the centre of South Australia, the former stop-off point for domestic planes flying across the continent and the home of Rosslyn 'Toss' Nitschke.

The Rankins had told me to make sure I saw Toss's father's baggy green cap. Slinger Nitschke played in the 1931–32 Australian Test cricket team, which included the great Donald Bradman. Toss opened the door in her dressing gown—a tall blonde woman with a strong voice and a friendly face. While she went to dress she invited me into the kitchen. Once Mount Eba was a small township consisting of dozens of staff for the rocket range, the Crombie family, a

Bill Stretton with his dingo scalps in the 1950s. Remains of his camps can still be found on the fence fifty years later.

book-keeper, governess, housemaid, cook and about thirty stationhands. Today there are three permanent staff and two casuals. I passed the dining room where Mrs Flo Crombie, whom Peter Morton describes as a 'Rabelaisian woman who was awed by no one', gained even greater notoriety in the late 1950s:

> Mount Eba was visited by no less a person than the governor-general, Field Marshal Sir William Slim. With some ceremony Slim and his party were ushered into the

old homestead with its fortress-like walls to keep the heat out, and thence to the cool and spacious dining room at the centre. They stared in wonderment at the ceiling lined with blue-painted canvas and the vast mahogany dining-room table capable of seating a couple of dozen. Slim was a distinguished soldier who had led the 14th, so-called 'forgotten', Army to a great victory in Burma. But he was very British, patrician, and somewhat stiff in manner. He made a valiant attempt to establish some rapport with his hostess, 'Well, well, Mrs Crombie, this is absolutely marvellous, marvellous. Here am I, in the middle of a desert, sitting at comfort at the head of your table.'

'My bloody oath you're not!' was Mrs Crombie's stout reply. 'My old man's the one who sits at the head of the table. You're down here.'

Toss had recently lost two working dogs to the 1080 poison baiting, designed to kill dingoes. A staff member had left baits too close to the homestead, which were then eaten by one of the dogs. That night when it was locked up it vomited as it died; the other dog ate the vomit and was also poisoned. Even with new precautions there is no guarantee that her dogs are safe. 'It's very hard to live with this poison bait—even the crows can move it close to the homestead.'

Toss also has several rockets but larger relics of this period are a kilometre away—derelict buildings which once contained top secret radar and computer technology. I could have wandered around all day looking at unplugged pieces of space-age machinery sitting alongside century-old rabbit traps. What had the young, brilliant rocket scientists sent to Mount Eba thought of the place? I had travelled 1500 kilometres to limber up for the shock of its isolation.

An hour later I arrived at Billa Kalina Station, the home of the Greenfield family and my meeting place with fence patrolman Keith Beelitz. There was just time for a quick sandwich with Lorraine Greenfield in her immaculate kitchen before Beelitz arrived and we had to head off. I had parked my car in the yard and left the doors and windows open to let some hot air escape. When I returned I discovered that my thermometer had exploded. A strange blue chemical was all over the passenger's seat after the bulb burst at the 50-degree Celsius mark. Amazingly, within fifteen minutes the stain had vanished—I assume it evaporated.

It was only twenty kilometres that Beelitz and I had to drive that day but the country was so rough it would require at least ten hours behind the wheel. I grabbed a few essentials and squashed into Beelitz's car, my knee pressed against his rifle. Beelitz had a sharp mind and a strong sense of curiosity—he had taken a moment to peer into my car window, noted my belongings and then asked me questions based on what he had seen.

Beelitz was fifty-nine years old and seemed the least likely-looking boundary rider that I had yet seen. Silvery-haired, slightly built, with a gentle face that you would expect to see in an office rather than the desert, he had been a clerk for eight years, a computer engineer for twenty-three, ten as a farmer and two and a half years on the Dog Fence. This was to be his final run. When we reached the fence he confessed, 'It's the sort of job that destroys your mind, driving along the same bloody fence repetitively every second week.'

The wire passed like static lines on a television set. 'When I first started I would be sleeping and see wire meshing flashing past,' Beelitz told me without taking his eyes off the fence. 'Sometimes you almost sense a hole before you actually see it. It does become slightly mesmerising—it's like being a cricketing fielder. You are standing there, standing there and then when the bloody ball does come you're not watching.'

All patrolmen have tales of driving past big holes in blissful ignorance. 'People's minds can create meshing where there is none. The fence can make you feel sleepy because it does have a slightly hypnotic effect.' Patrolmen call the condition 'hole blindness'.

The landscape was rough and coated in stones ranging from pebble-size to boulders. Beelitz had had his fuel tank reinforced for fear of a rock giving way and the chassis suddenly dropping onto a sharp stone. Tyres get shredded and even the toughest only last a few trips. This section is measured in kilometres per day instead of per hour. He is not paid a wage but a set amount per kilometre—$6.50. His total run is 286 kilometres. If there is work to be done then he must stop and do it—a significant job considering the numbers of kangaroos and emus that thrash and tear holes in the netting. After a heavy rain kilometres of the Dog Fence can be swept away and patrolmen must get in as soon as the mud has formed a crust strong enough to carry a vehicle.

The essence of Beelitz's contract is simple—the responsibility for keeping his run dog-proof is his alone. Like all South Australian fence patrolmen he is a contractor who tendered for his run and must supply his own four-wheel-drive, equipment, tyres, food and communications gear. The only exception to this is patrolmen privately employed by station owners to maintain some sections of the Dog Fence, such as Dean Jaensch. Added to all this patrolmen often find themselves the scapegoat for any perceived inadequacies in the fence structure. Some pastoralists have been known to deliberately not tell a patrolman about a hole to test whether it is detected. Beelitz is a sensitive man and these combined factors have left him with a sense of injustice. He sees maintenance as a strategy to prevent problems arising, whereas the resources of the Dog Fence Board really only allows them to be fixed. 'As a computer engineer you try and keep the computer going 99.9 per cent of the time, and my attitude is that you don't wait for a problem to occur, you nip it in the bud.'

Only once in two and a half years has he encountered

Keith Beelitz. 'Dingoes are such a vast problem that you need a vast solution.'

anyone else while on his run along this stretch of the fence. He has never met the patrolman to the west nor the man to the east. 'The chances of meeting the other bloke are one in a million because you are only at the beginning or the end for a couple of minutes.'

Everything about that gibber stretch was extraordinary because it was such a pristine environment. One of the most striking features of stony deserts is that in most places the top layer of rock is only a few stones deep. Beneath are heavily leached, impoverished sands sucked dry of every last nutrient. The gibber stones themselves looked as though they had been enamelled. I had not expected to see anything beautiful out here, yet day after day I had passed through magnificent deserts. I realised that in 1500 kilometres I had not seen a dingo or a single sheep within sight of the fence. Beyond the structure was cattle country or wilderness, yet I had not spotted a cow on the fence either.

That entire afternoon we drove with two parallel fences on our right: old abandoned stumps with hand-drilled holes put in place a century ago, and behind that the 'new' fifty-year-old fence which looks almost as ancient. The wood was exquisite, aged and smooth; splinterless, with curves and depressions that made each piece look as if it had been sculpted. If South Australian boundary riders have it tough today, a century ago their lives must have been miserable beyond imagination. The disused fence makes no concessions to geography, going up and over the steepest, rockiest ridges and hills, like the fin spines on the back of some bulging groper. No matter how steep the obstacle, no matter how thick the piles of gibber, those teams sunk the posts for the grazier. Labour then was so cheap that there was no need for the fence to take a more sensible route.

Just when it seemed as though the landscape could not become more picturesque two eroded peaks came into view, one of them known as Chinaman's Hat Hill, named by John

McDouall Stuart in 1858. We had arrived at the best time of day to observe them. I find mountains irresistible and wished I could spend a week exploring this area. I made a promise to myself that I would come back before it became a tourist destination with toilets, carparks, coaches, interpretive signs and guides. An hour later, in the last few minutes of light, we arrived on the Mudla Creek where giant coolibahs were catching the last rays of sun, which turned their leaves from green to bright yellow. There was barely time to lay out my gear before darkness turned the canopies of the trees into jagged black silhouettes against the Milky Way. The coals on the fire were glowing like iron in a blacksmith's forge when I realised Beelitz had built it using three 100-year-old fence-posts. 'There's a hundred and fifty posts for every kilometre, which means in the Greenfields' stretch alone there's fifteen thousand of them,' Beelitz said. Fenceposts may not be an endangered item in this region, but trees are.

Beelitz dropped me back at the Greenfields the next morning, though I was sure I would catch up with him again in the next two days.

As soon as I saw Keith Greenfield I liked him immensely. He is a stocky man with wild eyebrows, an easy but reserved smile, with a passion for history and fifty years' experience of the property he runs. He also understands that the greatest thanks a person can offer in return for the gift of life is to enjoy living. 'I am one of those fortunate people who has spent their whole working life doing exactly what they wanted to do.'

His parents had come to Billa Kalina as newlyweds in 1940 and Greenfield remembers the last of the Dog Fence inspectors who travelled by camel. He can still vividly recollect the camel trains of the early 1950s pouring into the station. Like most youngsters whose family run pastoral stations, he was sent to a city boarding school for his secondary education. He had to confront the immense gulf that exists between the city and the outback in Australia. His family property is 700,000 hectares and other students used to approach him and ask 'What do you need that much land for?' The Dog Fence cuts through his property—to the south is Millers Creek, 200,000 hectares that is home to 10,000 sheep. North of the fence, in dingo country, is the 500,000-hectare Billa Kalina where 3500 cattle live.

Greenfield's father declared Billa Kalina a nature reserve and instilled in his son a love of wildlife and the land. Even so, he was also a government scalp collector, authorised to pay bonuses for dead dingoes. Keith's great-grandfather was a shepherd. Lorraine Greenfield also has wire in her veins—she grew up on Murnpeowie Station.

In the Greenfields' 1950s vintage kitchen, Keith handed me a letter sent by historian and camel adventurer Phil Gee, who in 1993 had retraced Stuart's 1858 trek:

We are now quite sure that Stuart first entered Billa Kalina on the 28th June 1858, and that he passed your Chandlers WH (Dam) 2km to the north, heading in a westerly direction. He camped on the south side of Tent Hill. From here he veered to the NW and crossed the Emu Creek between the old Emu Well and your Newlyn Bore, camping on the night of the 29th on the very headwaters of the Ambulance Creek. The next day he headed straight for the RHS of the landmark called Prominent Point, leaving Billa Kalina country in the process.

On his return journey Stuart passed within twenty kilometres of the homestead.

At my excitement on reading this letter, Keith offered to show me where Stuart came through. A few minutes later we were thundering across Billa Kalina. The station has an average annual rainfall of nearly fourteen centimetres but it is almost always in what any other farmer would describe as drought. 'You have to work on the principle that the last rain is the last rain that you will have for years,' Keith told me. 'You have to work on the basis that every day could be the start of a drought.' To survive he and his father sent down bores in the artesian basin up to 120 metres deep. Windmills draw the liquid to the surface and it is stored in troughs and giant plastic tanks. It is this fossil water that fell as rain millions of years ago on Queensland's Great Dividing Range that keeps the pastoralists in business. As the rain fell thousands of kilometres away it soaked deep into the ground, eventually reaching the aquifers of the Great Artesian Basin. Over many millions of years it travelled below the continent. 'The water is just drinkable—but it will clean out any blockages in your system.'

When the rain does fall it is the gibber that provides life, for it funnels moisture into tiny pockets where vegetation is able to survive. 'I reckon this country grows the best-tasting beef in the world.'

In the car a familiar voice came on the two-way radio. It was Toss from Mount Eba talking to her staff about moving eighty sheep to another paddock. I felt as though I was leaving one life after another behind me and that by moving so quickly through the country the fence traverses I was missing many subtleties of the landscape and its people.

Keith Greenfield loves this land's spectacular desolation. 'In a lot of ways being here is like being out on the sea—the full horizons, the space,' he told me as we stood on the Dismal Plain. 'If I didn't live here I would be a sailor or a fisherman.' He and Lorraine had once taken a cruise and, late at night, out on the deck, this man of the desert realised that his home has a universal quality. 'Watching the swell in the moonlight was like camping out here on a moonlit night.'

Keith stopped the car and showed me Emu Creek and, behind it, Tent Hill where Stuart had passed a century and a half ago. The landscape shimmered and the heat was overpowering. How frightening it must have been to travel through such a place when you could never be certain where the next drink would come from. We headed to the old Emu Well, built twelve years after Stuart explored the area but now derelict. It was dug by a team of men using shovels and explosives until at some point, over 100 metres down, water flowed into the hole. What a delicious moment that must have been after weeks of backbreaking work. The well then had to be lined with timber, which was cut and milled locally. Emu was a government watering point, established for travellers between Tarcoola and the north–south railway. Greenfield's own uncle lost an arm doing such dangerous work. 'The men endured hardships that we cannot even imagine,' Greenfield said.

I made my farewells and was back on the Dog Fence track. Ahead of me was Roxby Downs—a prefabricated mining town that had sprung up in the late seventies after uranium and copper were discovered. At that point, however, I didn't care why the town was there as long as I could stock up on supplies, fix the tyre I had punctured on the way to the Twins and find somewhere to put my head down.

CHAPTER 7

THE CAT-PROOF FENCE

With its neat, new streets and modern homes Roxby Downs reminded me of Canberra coated with a dusting of paprika. The only reason for this city's existence is the Olympic Dam mine, and I expected to drive into a rusty town peopled by hard-bitten old miners. Instead, I was in a place full of young families. It was the closest I felt to home since leaving Sydney. I headed straight for the mall in the town centre. An hour after worrying that I was going to bog myself on a sand dune in the middle of nowhere, I was ordering a banana smoothie at a Wendy's franchise in the main drag of Roxby Downs. As I had driven into town I saw sand dunes hard up against the backyard fences of quarter-acre blocks with emerald-green lawns.

I hoped to meet with a team of young scientists based here, who are working to protect Australian fauna. In 1997 the South Australian National Parks and Wildlife Service, the University of Adelaide, volunteers and Western Mining

Corporation erected a cat, rabbit, dingo and fox-proof fence around sixty square kilometres of this sand dune country. Slowly the native animals that once lived there were reintroduced. More than ten kilometres of the boundary of the sanctuary, called the Arid Recovery Reserve, is made up of the Dog Fence, and I wanted to see how it could be used as a tool for conservation.

This is the largest area on mainland Australia from which rabbits have been removed. Once inside a feral-proof fence, native creatures are safe from predation and competition and often breed explosively. Tragically, though, sanctuaries like this are becoming the only place to see creatures such as bilbies, bettongs and bandicoots. Apart from kangaroos and emus, virtually all other large native life in central Australia has been eradicated from vast areas of their former ranges. But feral-proof fences only buy us some time. Unless noxious predators are exterminated and habitat degradation is reversed then the continent's ecosystems will become as bereft as the abandoned rocket range buildings at Mount Eba.

I sat in my car, waiting for Peter Paisley, a Western Mining Corporation employee, who over the phone offered me the three things I most wanted—dinner, a shower and a place to sleep. Paisley is a big, friendly guy, so tall that he had to re-fit his bathroom mirror nearly a foot higher to see his reflection. He is the double of one of my best friends so I instantly felt as though I had found not only a home for a night but a mate as well. After a three-course vegetarian meal Paisley took me back to the mall so I could meet local roo shooter Lindsay King.

King was sitting in near darkness on a park bench on a traffic island in the town centre, devouring an enormous hamburger and drinking flavoured milk. His day was just beginning—as the night cooled he would head out for several hours of kangaroo shooting. He would gut his catch out of town before dawn, providing a boon for local scavengers, and then send the chilled carcasses off to Adelaide to be sold for human consumption.

Roo shooters are another nocturnal creature of the outback and the Dog Fence is one of their favourite haunts. Most pastoral stations have at least one full-time roo shooter. At night two-way radios come alive as hunters discuss the shooting. It is a lonely and bloody existence, and when Paisley told King about plans to radio-collar half a dozen rabbits outside the sanctuary so he could monitor their movements, the roo shooter looked dumbstruck.

'What the fuck would Professor Dickhead want to study rabbits for?' He wasn't joking.

We arranged to talk over the radio through the evening and then climbed into Paisley's four-wheel-drive and headed into the desert.

Thirty minutes later I was back out on the Dog Fence with the sanctuary scientists. Paisley was armed with a .22

rifle and I had a fishing net. We used a spotlight from the back of the ute to search for rabbits outside the reserve. As soon as we spotted one the vehicle came to a jolting halt. Paisley raised his rifle and fired a bullet between the ears of the pest to stun it. Two of us jumped off and sped through the scrub as the rabbit bolted. The first rule of the net is that you aim it in front of the animal. Rabbit numbers are at a historic low, largely due to calicivirus, and it was not until 1.30 am that we had caught and collared the six animals that Anthony Pieck needed for his study. We had also seen three feral cats outside the sanctuary fence and Paisley shot one as it fled.

Up the road from the sanctuary, near William Creek, sits the Cat Tree. Here the public and shooters hang dead feral cats from an old mulga, and at any time there may be dozens of the stinking carcasses dangling like macabre Christmas decorations. Mummified cats even hang from signs on the road into Roxby.

I was desperately tired but Paisley wanted to show me inside the sanctuary at night-time. The young scientists drove back to Roxby while Paisley and I opened Jurassic Park-like gates into the reserve and entered a marsupial world that would make any cat-lover ashamed. My first impression was that there was a marsupial mice plague—they had not been reintroduced into the area but had taken advantage of the sanctuary's safety to explode in numbers and they hopped across our path at speed. The mesh that protects the reserve is three centimetres in diameter, which is small enough to keep even rabbit kittens out but not to prevent the mice from leaving. Paisley had a gecko to release and we saw two bilbies and two burrowing bettongs.

On the way back to Roxby, Paisley radioed through to King and asked him how his shooting was going. 'Pretty shithouse—I've only got forty so far,' was the reply. He told Paisley he was heading out near the Dog Fence to find a mob and asked whether I wanted to join him. All *I* wanted to do was stop for a few hours and give my brain and body a rest. At 3 am I finally fell asleep on my ground mat on a slab of concrete near Paisley's carport. At 6 am the scientists headed back out to the sanctuary. I planned to meet them at 9, which gave me enough time to refuel and organise my gear for the next stretch.

The scientists were on quad bikes at the base of a six-metre-high sand dune, preparing their gear and showing no signs of sleep deprivation. Over 800 species of plants are known to grow in this region and the sand ridge we were climbing that morning was covered in cane grass, hop bush and sandhill wattle. The vegetation was so thick that when my hat blew away it took me nearly half an hour to find it. The sand dunes themselves are a thriving ecosystem and house a strange amphibian—the trilling frog (*Neobatrachus centralis*) which lives most of its life beneath the dune's surface.

To be a frog in the desert is to be a creature of enormous patience, for rainfall fails to reach the average of 166 millimetres nearly two years out of three. It is possible that these creatures live in excess of thirteen years, feeding only three or four times a year. In severe periods of drought they feed only once every few years and sometimes get one chance in a decade to breed. In 1997, near Tibooburra and after heavy rains, I saw trilling frogs in such immense numbers that it was almost impossible not to step on them. Their tadpoles filled puddles in little black wriggling clouds. Trilling frog tadpoles can metamorphose within seventeen days, pumping the same hormone through their systems that induces premature births in humans. Snakes, foxes and cats are all known to feed on the adult frogs. In turn, the amphibians eat as many as thirteen different types of ants as wells as termites, spiders, beetles, and each other.

After rain back in October 2001, the scientists marked where seven trilling frogs were buried to find out more about what they do underground. Every few months since the frogs have been carefully excavated to measure their depth below the surface and their weight. There is no easy way to dig up a trilling frog, though a long arm helps. After twenty minutes or more of taking it in turns digging with Jude Carter, she produced a tiny frog the size of a fifty-cent piece, with membranes over its nose and mouth. It had a plastic, heavy, cold feel of a miniature, used, disposable nappy. The one we

A burrowing frog. It was tempting to splash water on it, but that would prematurely end its hibernation.

found was at a depth of 1.12 metres and measured 3.8 centimetres in length. A sand dune would never seem the same to me again—what other strange creatures were underneath our feet? There must be millions of these frogs waiting for the next downpour. Peter Paisley's colleague John Read estimates a conservative minimum of 200 individuals per hectare around Roxby Downs, making them the most abundant vertebrate in the area. The frogs are handled for as short a period as possible then carefully put back in their holes and reburied. It was time for me to move on and I wondered what I would find next along the Dog Fence.

Bill Sandow had told me not to drive the next leg of the fence, yet Keith Beelitz was up ahead and providing I was in his vicinity then I was safe. Sandow hadn't known that I would be following Beelitz's tracks and, anyway, it was too late to check with him now. Within an hour I had reached a range that looked down on the giant Lake Torrens.

It was easy to see how such an expanse of white inspires fear in some hearts but can have a siren-like call on others. When I first heard the story of Thomas Tuchyna, a twenty-six-year-old pilot who, in 1996, landed his rented Cessna on the lake, bogged himself and nearly died, I thought he was a fool. Tuchyna ended up walking fifteen kilometres from his plane. A day after his strange decision to land on the lake, which like all saltpans can be notoriously moist below its thin salt crust, a helicopter found him sheltering under a tree. Looking down on Torrens, I too felt drawn to walk on it.

I caught up with Beelitz at lunchtime. Once he reached the end of his run he would turn around for the last time and drive back to Whyalla. The look on his face as we said goodbye told me that he was saving his best farewell for the fence. I was now on my own until I reached the Oodnadatta Track near Marree. Soon I passed through painted desert country, with mountains coloured in every imaginable shade of ochre, including an albino peak that looked as though it had been built of chalk. There was not a sign of another human being. On the western side of the ridge that the track followed was the drainage for Lake Eyre and to the east the drainage for Lake Torrens. Then the landscape changed again.

Upon reaching Gregory Creek I felt as though I was in a mini Flinders Ranges. The Dog Fence was slung across a wide, sandy, dry waterway, held up by two mighty river red gums. The wire from the fence chewed into their boles, swelling the wood above and below, the same way that a finger reacts when string is tied around it too tightly. Soon after, I crossed Screech Owl Creek. Phil Gee says that here, in August 1840, Edward Eyre made one of the great mistakes of his exploration of the continent. For nearly two decades after Eyre's explorations people lived under the misconception that a horseshoe of salt lakes barred travel into the centre of the continent. He entered the Lake Eyre south drainage basin and thought he was ringed in by Lake Torrens to the south and Lake Eyre to the north. Eyre failed to climb a mountain just west of the Dog Fence to verify his findings.

Rain is rare in the Lake Eyre south drainage basin, but when it arrives it can bring with it the illusion of a land of milk and honey. In January 1864, five years after pastoral settlement of the region, drought came. The graziers had no idea how to manage it and the hopes of the new wave of settlers, who had followed in the footsteps of explorers like Stuart, were devastated. Many blamed Stuart himself. The explorer was the original lessee of a station on the current Dog Fence called Stuart Creek. He died in London in 1866 when the drought was at its worst. Investors lost hundreds of thousands of pounds and more than a quarter of a million sheep and 30,000 cattle perished. For the Scotsman who had led the first party to cross the continent and lived to talk about the experience it was an ignominious end.

At 5 pm I reached the old abandoned Ghan railway line where the Oodnadatta Track crosses Pole Creek. I had been so absorbed in my driving that I was relieved to discover one of the most hazardous parts of the track was now behind me. The Oodnadatta Track, which today is more like a highway, is one of the three most famous desert tracks in all of Australia, and in the next few days the Dog Fence would take me across the other two—the Strzelecki and the Birdsville. The three roads radiate out from the Marree/Mount Lyndhurst area like the bent spikes of a trident. These are three legendary outback routes, but on reaching the Oodnadatta after my drive from Roxby Downs, I felt I was back in civilisation. The first car made it into that part of the world in 1907. Generally, however, the mechanisation of central Australia only began in earnest with the post-World War II sales of ex-military four-wheel-drives. Over longer distances drovers moved stock, and dams were sunk using horses, bullocks or camels.

I decided to head into Marree, fifty kilometres down the Oodnadatta, and arrived there almost on dusk. It was deadly quiet. The baby-boomer silver nomads come through here but not in the height of summer. Marree has always been a place visited on the way to somewhere else. Today it is a spot to have a beer, refuel, look at some old memorials and pick up a few frozen chops from one of its two little shops.

I made my way back to Pole Creek, set up my camp a few hundred metres from the Oodnadatta Track and cooked dinner. Just as I was about to lift my chop from the frying pan to my plate I dropped it in the sand, turning it into a crumbed cutlet. The accident made me feel tired and homesick. I used a full cup of water to wash it and then ate it without enthusiasm.

I went to bed afraid, thinking of the Peter Falconio murder in central Australia earlier in the year, aware of the fact that this was the closest camp I had made to a main road. Before I left the next morning I walked across the abandoned Ghan railway bridge. Most Australians think that the name Ghan was given in honour of Afghan and Indian camel men, when in fact the commissioner of Commonwealth Railways was G. A. Gahan. The Ghan was built between 1884 and

1891 and with it came whole communities to keep it going, workers like the scoop-men who constantly laboured to keep the sand dunes from encroaching on the railway tracks. They have now all gone but the yards where they kept their animals are still to be found.

Lake Eyre is the largest salt lake in Australia and the third largest in the world, covering 9000 square kilometres. It has a catchment with tentacles that cover 1.3 million square kilometres—one sixth of the entire continent drains into this great white hole, as the lake is the lowest point in Australia. Belt Bay at the south-western end of Lake Eyre north is 15.2 metres below sea level. Once the saltpan was part of an even larger body of water called Lake Dieri, which was permanently filled from about 50,000 to 20,000 years ago. Dieri comprised the modern-day salt lakes of Eyre, Callabonna, Frome, Blanche and Gregory.

Once the water arrives in the lake from its tributaries it has nowhere to go and evaporates at the rate of 2.5 metres per year—more than twenty times the annual average precipitation. The salt is left behind and the sands that are carried into the lake from as far away as central Queensland are blown off into the surrounding deserts.

In April 1963 Donald Campbell, together with twenty-eight staff, arrived at Muloorina Station. He was there to break the land speed record on Lake Eyre in his space-age car, Bluebird. Also staying at the station were film crews, reporters, refuellers and Dunlop tyre experts. Over 100 army personnel were dispatched to Muloorina for crowd control. There were so many visitors on the property that a system of daily passes had to be implemented for those who wished to travel to the lake. There were strong winds and nearly eight centimetres of heavy rain and, after several weeks of preparations, the desert became a quagmire and the whole show had to be abandoned. For over a year the Bluebird was mothballed inside the Muloorina woolshed before Campbell and his team returned. On 17 July 1964, conditions were perfect. The car's gas turbines fired into life and the rocket-like vehicle hurtled across the salt lake, attaining a speed of nearly 650 kilometres per hour (403.1 mph).

In January 1974, Eyre had 400 millimetres of rain in two weeks, three times the annual mean. It was a record downfall, thought to occur only about once every 500 years. Scientists estimated that at its peak the lake held 32.5 million megalitres, which is over seventy times the volume of Sydney Harbour. The lake contains around 500 million tonnes of salt and when Edward John Eyre first saw what was to become his namesake in 1840, he was deflated. 'With bitter feeling of disappointment I turned from the dreary and cheerless scene around me.' For me, however, visiting its shores was a type of pilgrimage.

I arrived on a sand dune above the lake, brewed myself a coffee and stood there for half an hour savouring the stillness before walking down a dune and out onto the crackling, blinding lake bed. It was as if the sea had been sucked out, before the arrival of some great tsunami. I walked for more than a kilometre and I do not think that I have ever been in a quieter place. The only sounds I could hear were my breath and my shoes breaking the salt crust.

On my way back I stopped to read the Donald Campbell memorial commemorating the day when his machine had rewritten the record books. With Campbell's achievement humans had pushed through yet another technological barrier, during a decade that would culminate with a landing on the Moon. It was an event that Australians basked in—like the rocket range and nuclear testing, the land speed record was proof of our modernity.

In the year 2000 hundreds of thousands of people flocked to see Lake Eyre when it filled with water again. Yet the locals laugh about the 2000 flood, which in reality was not even 1974's baby sister.

Today Muloorina Station is owned by the Mitchell family. It is one of the few properties that has sheep outside the Dog Fence—its shearing sheds are north of the fence. As a consequence of this much of the testing of new fences is undertaken here. Muloorina is also fast becoming a popular tourist destination: an area near the wetland behind the homestead is offered as a free campsite and has become a birdwatcher's paradise. On the day I was there clouds of corellas were as thick as flies.

By the end of that afternoon I had followed the Dog Fence around to the Birdsville Track. On the way I encountered my second cocky gate and despite Wayne Rankin's instructions I could not see how it was possible to open it. Instead I disassembled the gate and put it back together again as best as I could.

That night I was planning to meet up with Shane Oldfield, the owner of Clayton Station—a cattle property on the Birdsville Track, north of the Dog Fence. (This station was the first in the region to have television transmission—a fuzzy image from a satellite back in 1980.) As I headed up the track I could see a plume of dust coming towards me. A ute appeared from within the cloud. It stopped alongside and a young man wearing a cowboy hat asked me if I was James Woodford. It was the first time I had heard someone say my full name in nearly three weeks. 'Shane's in town,' he told me, 'having a few beers at the Marree Hotel.'

Once again a strange South Australian settlement had me in its orbit. In half an hour I was back in Marree after a twelve-hour drive away from it. I believe this was testament to three things—the winding nature of the Dog Fence, the terrible condition of the Dog Fence track and the reluctance of people in isolated towns ever to let you leave.

CHAPTER 8

LAKE FROME

The size of the Marree Hotel is proof of how important beer is to the town. It is a grand and traditional outback pub of two storeys, with a verandah that runs the entire length of the top floor. Parked out the front were a dozen battered four-wheel-drives and several newer models belonging to tourists. Two kelpies obediently sat outside. Inside, the main drinking bar seemed small and crowded, but behind the cockies and workers I could see a maze of corridors and stairs leading to old billiard rooms and bedrooms.

Nervous and overawed by the sea of tough faces, I introduced myself to Shane Oldfield, a rugged wiry character, who seemed to be an important Marree identity. I asked him what he thought about the Dog Fence, especially the new waist-high electric fence on the southern boundary of Clayton Station. 'The best thing since sliced bread,' he said. 'I've got half the dogs I once had.' With the old netting fence, he explained, dingoes couldn't get through and they would congregate up against the wire. Now, according to Oldfield, they pass over or between the electrified wires. 'When seasons get dry in the Simpson they feed down towards the south. They used to come up hard against the fence and stop there until they took a bait, got stuck in a trap or we shot them. Now I haven't got half the problem. I reckon the dingo is a beautiful animal in his own right but when it gets dry and they're having trouble finding food they can be a problem.'

I asked him if he knew the next grazier that I wanted to meet, Michael Sheehan of Moolawatana Station. 'He's right next door,' Oldfield replied. As luck would have it that day all the graziers in the Lake Eyre south drainage basin had attended a meeting across the hall to discuss water management. In 1977, 86 billion litres of water was wasted from 200 bores in South Australia—the water came to the surface at the wells and poured across the desert, creating artificial wetlands and havens for feral animals. No one understands how long the resource can last and what the level of sustainable usage is. By 1996, through a program of capping and rehabilitating old bore sites, the loss had been nearly halved to 48 billion litres, yet this is still a staggering amount of water. The meeting was to discuss plans to see even greater controls on artesian water, perhaps even a bill for its use. Everyone whom I was planning to call on in the next few days was in that room—it was a one-stop cocky shop.

I pulled up a chair behind Michael Sheehan and waited

until he noticed me. We soon started talking about the possibility of me driving along the section of the Dog Fence that
runs through his property. Sheehan gave me permission and
instructions on how to make it through. There was only one
'really hairy' location: a place where the track goes down the
face of a steep slope and where, he guaranteed, the driver's-
side wheels would leave the ground for a few seconds when I
took one of the corners. 'No one has ever tipped over yet
though,' Sheehan said with a smile. 'And if you do, you'll only
roll once or twice. The most important thing is that if you
start to feel the car tipping, don't stop, because if you do then
you *will* roll your car.' Right.

'If it rains in there,' he went on, 'you could get stuck for a
couple of weeks, so make sure you stock up on food and
water before you leave.' This was worrying advice, because at
this time a big low pressure system was moving across the
centre of the continent.

I was invited to join a barbecue being cooked under the
vast verandah at the front of the pub. There were the ubiqui-
tous sausages and mutton but I looked at two bowls of salad
with such lust that no one dared stand between me and the
roughage that my body demanded.

Oldfield invited me to stay at a camping ground near his
station. I drove back along the Birdsville Track past Lake
Harry, towards what I had hoped would be a long soak in a
hot artesian spa. Before dawn, plagued by mosquitoes, I

decided to take a hot artesian shower. I must have done something wrong because within seconds of turning on the tap, water started pouring through the roof of the shower block, soaking a rare set of clean clothes and leaving me shivering. It was time to leave.

This time I achieved escape velocity and was soon back on the Dog Fence. I had finally started to master the cocky gates and I took great pleasure in manipulating the intricate levers devised to make these flimsy structures strong. I stopped to boil up a coffee and a little wagtail (*Rhipidura leucophrys*) twirled and swirled a few feet away, chasing invisible insects. The bird lifted my spirits and reminded me of home. The species is found across the continent and my favourite thing about them is that they can call all through the evening. When I wake in the middle of the night and my family is asleep, I listen to the wagtail's song. In the morning I am never sure whether I dreamed the melody or it actually happened. Minutes later I saw brumbies—a stocky stallion in magnificent condition led his four mares across the plain on the other side of the fence and I watched them in full nostril-flared flight.

At 10.20 am I saw my first dingo. He was a big golden male, healthy with a thick straw-coloured coat. His snout and paws were pale white. In almost two long weeks of driving this was the first wild dog I had seen. He unexpectedly appeared 100 metres in front of the car, and for a while trotted along the outside of the fence while I followed behind. He then headed into the saltbush where he stopped and turned around to look at me. Through my binoculars I watched him throw back his head and give three magnificent howls before he vanished.

Seeing this creature sealed an ongoing debate I have had with myself for years. I finally decided that dingoes *are* a part of the Australian fauna—they may be relative 'newcomers' but they are also highly adapted native wolves. The way he threw his head back and howled was haunting and beautiful—not the call of a feral pest. The sound was delayed by the wind and the distance, so his cry arrived out of sync with the opening of his mouth.

Every minute the sky was looking more and more threatening and when I reached the Strzelecki I even considered heading back to Marree. Once I left that last outback road it was the Flinders Ranges or bust. The weather was predicted to worsen so I made a push for Moolawatana before heavy rains made the Dog Fence track impassable. It was cool enough for me to consider putting a jumper on.

When I concentrate my tongue pokes out of my mouth and by the time I reached the base of the first ridge I had nearly bitten it off. The rest of that afternoon I was focused on precipitous, rocky tracks and sandy washaways, determining which were the old abandoned dog fences and which was the new. Each old fence has its own network of tracks and gates and nothing is signposted. In places the road has been washed or blown away, or giant rocks have risen to the surface. Sometimes it is not until you are right on top of these obstacles that you discover you have missed a detour. This stretch was also one of only a few places along the South Australian fence where the maintenance track moved, without warning, from 'outside' country to 'inside'.

Sheehan had told me that I would know when I reached the dangerous part of the fence. He was right, except there wasn't one place that appeared impassable, there were three— all within a couple of hundred metres. I was on top of an escarpment and the track weaved down the rise, rocky and uneven. I got out of the car and I could see that the boundary rider had recently passed because scraps of tyre tracks were visible in the sand between piles of sharp rubble. I hopped in the car, squeezed the steering wheel, clenched and contorted my face as if executing a clean and jerk weightlift, and began to roll along the slope. I felt my driver's-side wheels lifting off the ground and then heard an Aussie version of Obi-Wan Kenobi's voice, aka Michael Sheehan's, saying: 'The most important thing is that if you start to feel the car tipping, don't stop, because if you do then you *will* roll your car.'

My heart felt like a big pounding soggy plum at the back of my throat, and then my side wheels lowered and all four tyres were back on the track. There was no going back now and I passed the other two danger points to reach the summit.

From there I could see one of the most famous landmarks in Australian exploration, Mount Hopeless. When Eyre saw the view from the summit he felt imprisoned by the expanse of salt lakes that sprawls across the desert at the northern end of the Flinders Ranges. The doomed Burke and Wills unsuccessfully struck out for Mount Hopeless from their base on the Cooper Creek.

Beside the Dog Fence was a cairn which seemed to mark this as the highest point of the maintenance track. Below me on the plain that surrounded the mountain range I could see a dry riverbed filled with green gums and I decided to make that my camp for the evening. An hour later I was on the banks of the dry Yerilla Creek in the most peaceful and comfortable spot I had visited so far.

All that day I saw animals, mountains, ruins and trees which had taken me completely by surprise. The river red gums, many hundreds of years old, each had cavernous hollows, essential for the survival of many of the continent's tree-dwelling mammals. I wished I had a proper spotlight with me to investigate what emerged from those holes after dark.

By the time I went to bed the sky was almost black with storm clouds. At midnight it started to spit and at 2.30 am rain began falling, forcing me to pack and make a run for Moolawatana. I drove for two hours, until I knew I was close to the next public road, before pulling my ground mat out for a short nap.

When I woke I felt as though I was not alone, and as I rolled over and looked under the chassis of the car, I saw eight legs on the other side—two dingoes. I stood up, expecting that by the time I walked around the car the dogs would be gone. They were pups, and by late summer they are weaned and start to wander. It is animals of this age that farmers find particularly troublesome. Both of the dingoes were bitches, only a little above knee-height, and they looked hungry. I called to them—one slinked off, the other started to head towards me then thought better of her decision and trotted after her sister.

Michael Sheehan was interviewed for a book called *Fence People* in the late 1980s. At that time he declared:

> There's plenty of room outside the Dog Fence for dingoes. A lot of people get the idea that dingoes are becoming extinct but there's more dingoes now than before white man came here. If they want to talk like that they should come and live out here. They sit down in their airconditioned offices and pontificate—it doesn't impress me at all. That's all a dingo is—a domestic dog gone wild. The Abos let him go wild four thousand years ago. People try to make them out to be something special, but they're just a dog. A nice-looking dog, but they'll kill just like any other dog, and they're no smarter than any other dog.

Michael Sheehan's opinion of dingoes has softened since he swapped sheep for cattle.

In 1991 more than 900 dingoes were shot, poisoned and trapped on Moolawatana, over ninety of which were inside the fence. Sheehan lost 3000 sheep in twelve months and nearly went bankrupt. 'They were killing sheep while we were trying to shear.'

Interestingly, Sheehan used to be a boundary rider along 115 kilometres of fence, but quit in disgust at the way the fence was managed, the lack of resources and because patrolling took up all of his time.

As I sat in his kitchen he told me he now only kills dingoes when they are causing problems. Today he runs cattle and the morning I arrived he had shot a dingo pup that had a calf bailed up. He wounded it with his rifle and finished it off with a pistol. 'They breed dogs today and they're just toys,' Sheehan told me. 'But when you see the real thing they're just beautiful—they're so tough and strong they can bring down an animal three times their size.'

The biggest dingo Sheehan ever saw weighed 30 kilograms. I related my troubles with the cocky gates and how dumb they had made me feel. His silent reply was to hold up a hand with four-and-a-half fingers. A cocky gate had severed one of his digits at the top knuckle. When Sheehan got home after this accident his wife Audrey sent their son Gerard to check the gate was closed. He found the chopped-off piece of finger, but ants had already started to devour it. Sheehan does not consider this a serious incident, particularly when compared to that of his son back in 1984 when the Royal Flying Doctor Service saved Gerard's life.

Sheehan related that story to Dinah Percival and Candida Westney in *Fence People*:

He had a bad asthma attack and stopped breathing for five minutes. He was dead; he was lying on the office desk not breathing. I was trying to give him mouth-to-mouth but it was hopeless. The doctor said, 'Have you got any oxygen?'

I said, 'Only industrial oxygen, on the oxy-acetylene equipment.'

'Get it!'

And I dragged the acetylene hose off, and dragged the oxygen down, and put the cutting torch in his mouth, and filled him up with oxygen. That did the trick—he started breathing. He went from black to pink, and in thirty minutes he had regained consciousness.

Before the oxygen had run out the flying doctor arrived from Port Augusta, hundreds of kilometres to the south. The doctor's hair was still wet when he walked into the homestead; he had taken the emergency call while he was in the shower.

Gerard now works on the station and Sheehan's daughter Jane is a stud overseer with a big pastoral company called Stanbroke—the biggest landholders in the nation. Like many children in central Australia both were taught to read and write by their mother.

Waking at Arkaroola, I heard the drone of an old aircraft above the settlement. Soon an antique Auster came into view and circled above me. I could see a face looking down through the window and, as I waved, Doug Sprigg dipped one of his wings in welcome. In 1962 the Sprigg clan became the first to cross the Simpson Desert in a motor car. At the time Doug—named after close family friend and Antarctic explorer Sir

Douglas Mawson—was only seven years old. Photos taken at the time show a moon-faced little boy, wearing glasses and always peering at something. Sprigg's mother, Griselda, who died in 2003, was a proud and adventurous matriarch.

An hour later and Sprigg arrived at Arkaroola. He is no longer moon-faced and chubby but lean and small. He is long-sighted, which gives his eyes a wise old-owl look, and he is widely regarded as the smartest man on the fence. Around 63,000 hectares in size, Arkaroola was once a pastoral property overrun by feral goats; today it is a nature and geological reserve.

Sprigg and I took off in his little Auster at around lunchtime. It is a *real* aeroplane—covered originally in Irish linen, now with dacron. It has all the levers and buttons and gauges of half a century ago and Sprigg is clearly an exceptional pilot. He mumbled aloud his checklist and then hand-started the wooden propeller, which spluttered to life like a cold, flooded lawnmower. Taking off felt as though we were soaring away on the back of a big furry moth—it was such a slow and gentle lift. We flew over Arkaroola Station and then Wooltana, which neighbours the Dog Fence, before heading out of the Flinders Ranges and across the red dusty country that fills the 30-kilometre-wide plain between the Flinders Ranges and Lake Frome. Sprigg gave me the controls of the Auster on the approach to Lake Frome. It was the first time that I had ever flown an aeroplane. The salt lake was in front of me and I kept the nose of the Auster just below its western edge, surprised at how responsive the controls were.

Lake Frome is so white that it is used by a number of satellites to calibrate their instruments as they orbit overhead. In 2000, scientists determined that its reflectivity is around 70 per cent—the moon by comparison has a reflectivity of 7 per cent.

Before leaving for the fence I had interviewed Dean Graetz at the CSIRO's Earth Observation Centre in Canberra. He told me that Lake Frome may be one of the brightest places on Earth. In 2001 a NASA satellite orbited at an altitude of 700 kilometres directly above the surface of Lake Frome, measuring the amount and colour of reflected light. At the same moment, on the lake's surface, Graetz's team also measured the light. These results will contribute to new mapping techniques, crucial to understanding our planet.

'In terms of sunlight hours and brightness, Lake Frome beats Antarctica hands down,' Graetz said. 'The southern end of the lake is the brightest, brighter than clouds or snow. It is so reflective that it is black in the infra-red.'

One of the main reasons that Frome is so valuable to the scientists is that it doesn't only reflect light. 'If you shine a torch on a mirror it will reflect light without it being scattered,' Graetz explained. 'But on Frome you feel as though light is generating underneath you, you feel as though the salt is glowing. You feel as though the lake is generating the light.

This is because of the vast range of surfaces on the lake—the fact that the salt crystals are so rough and because all over Frome there are infinite little formations, waves of salt, broken crusts and islands that all scatter light.'

I have flown over the Antarctic ice cap in summer but the salt lake below me was far more dazzling than that. It is whiter than a baby's tooth or the top of a cloud. Once my eyes got used to the brightness I could see that Frome is far from featureless. There were patterns and shapes in the salt that reminded me very much of polar sea-ice. We flew towards some islands in the middle of the 150-kilometre-long lake. Doug pointed out sweeping grey lines around the islands. These parallel smudges are lines formed from tens of millions of salt-mummified locusts that were blown onto the lake a few years ago. The islands themselves were created over thousands of years as sediment was blown onto the surface of the lake and slowly collected around ridges in the salt.

Sprigg then flew right into the heart of the Flinders wilderness, including a pass over the Mawson Plateau, one of the most isolated ecosystems on the continent. Apart from helicopter the only way to reach the plateau's clear, black pools is by several days of arduous hiking.

When we returned Sprigg showed me a dining table-sized satellite image of Frome—from space the expanse of salt looked like a giant teardrop. The islands were also visible, but the most spectacular thing about the photograph was to see the impact the Dog Fence has had on the continent's environment.

Grazing is not the only reason vegetation is ravaged inside the fence. The absence of dingoes means that kangaroo populations are at unnaturally high levels. Sprigg ran his finger along the fenceline. 'Outside of the fence you can see much more vegetation than there is below it.'

Pastoralists say the 'fence effect' is caused by the extra grazing pressure put on vegetation by the enormous numbers of kangaroos inside the fence. Environmentalists and an increasing number of scientists, however, say it is because sheep overgraze these areas. The most vocal scientific critic of the impact of sheep in the outback is national parks scientist Daniel Lunney.

'It was sheep, and the way the land was managed for the export wool industry, that drove so many of the mammal species to extinction,' Lunney wrote in a recent scientific paper. 'The impact of ever-increasing millions of sheep on all frontages, through all the refuges, and across all the landscape by the mid-1880s, is the primary cause of the greatest period of mammal extinction in Australia in modern times.'

The truth is hard to test scientifically and there has never been a comprehensive national study of the ecological impacts of the Dog Fence. There has, however, been a long-running study into kangaroo and emu numbers on both sides

of the fence in the part of South Australia I was now travelling through. A team from the University of Queensland and
the University of New England conducted aerial surveys
between 1978 and 1992 and found that there is indeed a
'fence effect'. 'Lower densities of red kangaroos and emus
outside the dingo-exclusion fence in three distinct pastoral
regions of South Australia support the assertion...that this is
the result of dingo predation.' This study was restricted to
creatures big enough to be counted from a low-flying
aeroplane. Considering the length of the fence, the diversity
of ecosystems it traverses and the extremes of climate that the
central Australian landscape is subjected to, more subtle
impacts would take years of study.

Sprigg's satellite photo shows the territory between the
Flinders Ranges and the New South Wales border, and the
difference between one side and the other along the entire
fence was marked. The greatest contrast was between the last
two South Australian stations—Quinyambie, outside the
fence, and Mulyungarie, inside, and which was stripped bare
in comparison.

In his book *Red Sand Green Heart* John Read asserts that
'the Dog Fence is a magnificent tribute to our pioneers'. Yet
its historical importance may well be discounted because of
the damage it does to the environnment. Read concedes that
the job of the fence is to exclude dingoes from a third of the
continent, but he also writes: 'Dingoes serve the same role of

You're crossing...

THE DOG FENCE

| IS COOBER PEDY | OODNADATTA 183 |

This 5,600 km fence runs from Surfers' Paradise, Qld. to the Bight near WA Dingoes are found to the north - in cattle country. Protected sheep country is to the south.

For more information: UNDERGOUND BOOKS COOBER PEDY 086 725558

ne of the few places where the Dog Fence is signposted for tourists is near Coober Pedy in outh Australia.

The fence as seen from Doug Sprigg's Auster near Lake Frome. Every kink in the South Australian fence has now been recorded on GPS.

The dunes of the Strzelecki Desert are always on the move and pose the biggest problem for New South Wales fence patrolmen.

'On Frome you feel as
though the lake is generating
the light...waves of salt,
broken crusts and islands
that all scatter light.'
Dean Graetz

On Lake Frome with
an ants' nest in
the foreground.

Peter Flegg leans against the Queensland fence. 'I'd like to say the fence is effectively dog-proof. It keeps the honest dogs out.' The New South Wales fence is behind him (far left).

Fleggy working in dust near the Wilson River overflow.

male dingo in its prime strung from the Dog Fence near Hamilton Gate.

Rough country along the Dog Fence west of Thargomindah in Queensland.

One of the smaller mobs of frantic emus in front of Jerry Stanley's four-wheel-drive.

ot everything can fly through the netting like finches. The fence traps everything from echidnas
o ducklings.

Fleggy inspects a section of the Barrier Fence in Queensland.

Dusk on the fence just west of Hamilton Gate.

keeping foxes and feral cats in check in Australia as wolves and coyotes do in America. Dingoes not only compete with, but also kill cats and foxes. Where dingoes are abundant there are usually few feral predators.'

That night Sprigg hosted a barbecue. The chef was an old mate of Phoompy Price's, and also present were two British members of the Mars Society just arrived at Arkaroola. They were planning to assess the reserve's likeness to the red planet. The end of the South Australian fence was now within grasp and, by my reckoning, I would be in New South Wales in three days. There were no more rocky stretches ahead of me in South Australia but I did have to get through some big sand dunes at the bottom of Quinyambie Station at the southern end of Strzelecki. I had been told they were second only to those at Lake Everard in size.

In his space observatory Sprigg showed us Alpha Centauri—the next closest sun after our own. We saw the open cluster Theta Carina, the absorption and emission nebulae Eta Carina and the globular cluster 47 Tucanae. The cluster 47 Tucanae is 20,000 light years away and to the naked eye it looked like a single star, but through the telescope lens it was clear it is made up of millions of suns. I had followed the Dog Fence for over 2000 kilometres—a significant distance—and yet on a larger scale I had scarcely moved at all.

The next morning I decided to visit the Paralana Hot

Springs. A sign warns visitors not to swim. 'These waters are heated by hot rock at shallow depths, and by radioactive mineral decay. Carbon dioxide, nitrogen, radon gas and helium bubble forth continuously.' This permanent flow of water had created a dense little strip of forest from which constant noise emanated. The local Adyamathanha Aborigines call the site Vadaardlanha, which means 'dead finish fire'. 'Dead finish' is the wattle species *Acacia tetragonophylla*, a ferociously spiky shrub. I disturbed a wallaroo, whose shadow I could discern disappearing up the gorge. From out of the kelp-brown algae that covered the floor of the spring appeared gassy, hypnotic bubbles. The water was too hot to leave a finger in for more than a few seconds. Scientists now believe that it was in such a place, billions of years ago, that heat, radiation, chemistry and chance danced together and made life.

Since leaving Ceduna one name came up again and again along the South Australian fence—Alec Wilson. Everyone had suggested that I steer clear of him as he despises city visitors and has waged a long-running battle with four-wheel-drivers wishing to use a shortcut through his property to New South Wales. What fascinated me, though, is that he is a Dog Fence celebrity. Since the mid-1970s Wilson has acted in an assortment of movies, including *Crocodile Dundee II* and *III*,

Snowy River II, and *The ANZACs* mini-series. He has also appeared in beer ads. I called him the morning I left Arkaroola and asked if I could pop by his home at Frome Downs in the afternoon. His property of 6000 square kilometres backs onto a long stretch of the Dog Fence and I wanted to drive there without fear. He sounded suspicious and gruff, but I have often found that tough characters are easy to get along with if you are open with them.

Wilson told me to approach his homestead slowly to avoid running over one of his dogs. Someone else I met had been given a similar warning by Wilson. That person had approached the homestead at about 30 kilometres per hour— a speed deemed excessive by Wilson who ordered the visitor off his property. I made a mental note to drive up at ten kilometres per hour.

When I arrived, at 4 pm, Frome Downs seemed deserted. I walked through a gate towards an old, run-down homestead, with a chair on the verandah which looked as though it had been a seat for the viewing of thousands of sunsets. Under it were two pairs of well-worn thongs and an ashtray full of cigarette butts. I banged on the door a few times and then retreated to my car. A cheerful but wary young woman with an American accent appeared on her pushbike. 'What can we do for you?' she asked.

'I'm here to see Alex,' I replied.

'He's down at the main house.'

I drove on further to find a beautiful homestead. In the garden was an attractive woman in her late thirties, hanging out washing. I suddenly felt that the stories about Wilson might have been exaggerated. She gave me the most welcoming smile I had seen for weeks. 'I'm here to see Alex.'

'Alec,' she replied, correcting me with a politeness that disarmed me even further. 'I'm Deb, Alec's wife.' We went inside and she asked me to wait in the kitchen while she fetched her husband. When Wilson walked into the room he took my hand and squeezed it as though he was trying to pull it off. He was a rugged-looking, heavily built man with thick black hair, beginning to turn salt and pepper. He oozed attitude and had a presence that could be intimidating. He wanted to know why I was travelling along the fence.

Before I could answer a nervous Telstra technician appeared in the doorway. 'I want the new type of telephone system,' Wilson told him bluntly.

'That would be very expensive,' the technician said.

'I don't care, just rip the old one out and put the new one in.'

Deb laid out a plate of seven biscuits with pink icing and hundreds of thousands. Alec ate six of them before he said, 'You're making me feel like a pig. Aren't you going to have one?'

I picked up a biscuit, but because I was still cooling down from the heat outside I struggled to eat it. There were none

Alec Wilson on set
in *Crocodile Dundee III*.

left for the telephone guy, who stood around looking
awkward then made his excuses and left.

I told the Wilsons how impressed I was by Lake Frome. 'I
hate it. It's a boring waste of space,' Wilson said, his eyes
chiselling into my forehead. I looked across at Deb to see if
she agreed with her husband. She did. I changed the subject to
movies, and Wilson became bashful until I confessed that I
had not seen *Crocodile Dundee II* or *III*.

The phone rang and Wilson disappeared. Deb said she would show me her horses. She has her own quarterhorse breeding stud, complete with a new semitrailer rig to transport her stock all over the continent. Back out in the heat Deb seemed at home, and her horses crowded around like old friends. A gorgeous little brumby filly came up to us. She had been found by a stationhand a few days earlier and delivered to the homestead slung over the back of a motorbike. Brumbies are a major feral pest in the region and do immense damage to the landscape, but because they are herbivores they are largely ignored by pastoralists—although they compete with sheep they do not eat them.

Once we were back inside Wilson offered to show me some of his rifles. He came back with an 1873 Winchester. 'If you want to touch it, don't touch the metal,' he cautioned. Wilson brought out two more nineteenth-century Winchesters. The phone rang again and he disappeared, leaving me to look at three rifles I wasn't allowed to touch. He came back twenty minutes later. 'You can touch them if you want. Go on, pick one up—feel how much lighter that one is.'

The phone rang yet again and, armed with a photo of Alec and Deb's business card, I said my farewells and left.

It had been four nights since I last camped by the fence. I decided to drive on past Frome Downs and into Quinyambie—the last station on the South Australian Dog Fence. I found a small claypan ten metres from the fence and

One of the loneliest spots in Australia is the South Australia–New South Wales junction of the fence.

heated up a can of soup. That night the wind howled so hard that my sleeping bag flapped like an untrimmed sail, but the gale did not drown out the sound of dingoes howling or the noises of sticks breaking and footpads dragging on sand around my camp.

I woke gritty-eyed from lack of sleep but by mid-morning I had reached the New South Wales border and was thrilled. I stopped and touched the mesh at the corner, where the South Australian fence and the New South Wales fence meet, and thought back to when I had snipped a few centimetres of wire 2173 kilometres earlier.

I climbed back into the car and began to drive, registering the sight of something just ahead of me sticking up out of the sand. Metres later the four-wheel-drive made an enormous cracking sound and slammed to a halt. What I had spotted was actually the tip of a five-metre-long wire berg, the entire length of which was now wrapped around my drive shaft. It took me four hours to snip through the last piece of steel knot with my wire cutters and drive on.

CHAPTER 9

THE FAMOUS FENCE

Randall Crozier, the manager of Quinyambie, walked into the station's dining hall and rolled a handful of fossils across the table like dice. 'I found a dinosaur today,' he said to his kids. He had discovered a pile of bones in a swale between sand dunes in an area of his 12,000-square-kilometre property he had never before visited. When I showed a piece to scientist Tim Flannery a couple of months later, however, he identified it immediately as fossilised lightning—when a bolt sears into a dune it melts the sand, fusing it into cylindrical, rib-like stone. So rather than millions of years old the relics could be as recent as the last thunderstorm.

Quinyambie Station is immense, and to check his top border means a 400 kilometre round trip for Crozier. Its fences enclose such a tough desert landscape that throughout its entire length there are only two watercourses—Yandama Creek and Tilcha Creek, both of which can be dry for years at a time.

Forty-four-year-old Crozier is stocky and as tough-looking as a piece of gristle, but I soon learned why he is a favourite employee of one of the world's great grazing empires, the Kidman Pastoral Company. When Crozier walked into the room everyone instantly became happier. His wife Tanya loves him, his children idolise him, his station-hands and staff treat him with respect, and when he shook my hand he looked me square in the eye. Crozier is proud of Kidman's, which first employed him when he was fourteen. 'I felt like that was my home.' No one had made life easy for Crozier. He was born with a club foot and spent three years in Sydney to have his disability corrected. Most of his neighbours inherited their right to manage a slab of central Australia; Crozier has earned his.

In 2001, three decades later, Quinyambie was Kidman's station of the year. 'My job is to make sure I pass on the property in better condition than when I got it.'

Once the property used to support 14,000 head of cattle. Today, in an effort to reduce damage to the environment, stock numbers have been reduced to a high of 11,500.

Quinyambie has one of the highest densities of dingoes anywhere on the continent and on the day I arrived Crozier had seen nine but shot none. In recent years there has been a push to move the Dog Fence further north, bringing Quinyambie inside—a move which Crozier bitterly opposes. Dingoes keep roo numbers down and that's how Crozier likes it. Altogether he has 200 kilometres of Dog Fence, half of it along Quinyambie's southern boundary and run by the South Australians. The other half runs along the New South Wales border, the property's eastern boundary and is an impressive fence two metres high.

The head stockman, Lance, wearing a ten-gallon hat and riding boots held together with grey gaffer tape, joined us for a beer before dinner. In spite of the vastness of the property Lance knew where almost every mob of cattle was, and told Randall he had seen sixty-eight beasts at the last watering point he had visited that day. A spherical rocket fuel tank serves as the station bell and the entire Crozier family and all the staff—gyrocopter pilot, stationhands, governess and contractors—sat around an enormous table. By the time we had finished eating our stew and talking it was nearly 10 pm.

After everyone had washed their own dishes, smoked their final cigarette and downed their last beer, the lights began to turn out and the darkness of the surrounding Strzelecki drifted into the station like a fog. One of the last lights to go out was that of the governess Miss Melissa, who had only been there for a month. As I went to bed I smiled at how ten-year-old Ben Crozier had looked Miss Melissa in the eye over dinner and asked, 'When are you going to fall in love with one of the stationhands?'

She blushed, as did all the stationhands who took to

shovelling down mouthfuls of stew. 'That's what has happened to all our governesses,' Ben continued. 'Every one of them has fallen in love with a stationhand.'

Ahead of me was 269 kilometres of Dog Fence, heading straight up the 141st parallel to Cameron Corner. Fifteen kilometres along the New South Wales fence I came to Carol and Wally Egerer's home. Crozier suggested I stop in on them to let them know I would be driving along the border that day. Some years ago a patrolman was nearly killed when a tourist sped over a sand dune and ran him down. It is for this reason that the public is banned from the road running along the New South Wales fence unless they have a signed permit.

Wally has been an employee of the New South Wales Wild Dog Destruction Board for seven years, and is responsible for sixty kilometres of fence. 'I love the isolation,' Egerer told me. 'You're on your own. I like the quietness of it all, getting away from the rat race.' Unlike his South Australian counterparts he is paid a wage and given a house, a car and a flexi-day once a month. His home could have been lifted from the suburbs of any Australian city and is fitted out with everything needed to make life comfortable. All of his expenses are met by the board and the extra money shows—the fence is a great wall of wire which looks as if it could stop an army. It is in perfect condition and a dirt highway runs along beside it.

The New South Wales fence is owned and run by the state government. Considerably shorter than both the South Australian and Queensland stretches of the Dog Fence, it nevertheless receives more money for its maintenance. Inside the fence, too, farmers are more committed to the structure, largely because on the outside lurk some of the highest dingo numbers in Australia.

Heading north, the Strzelecki Desert's red sand dunes roll unbroken for hundreds of kilometres. A strong wind blew the grains of sand like spume at the crest of a storm swell. By lunch I had reached the old abandoned Quinyambie homestead. Until the arrival of calicivirus it served as a base for rabbiters. I wondered what stories had soaked into the derelict homestead's thick, insulating walls. I could imagine children being raised, mothers holding their home together during droughts that lasted years, and floods that turned the Strzelecki Desert into an inland ocean. The Dog Fence is a few hundred metres from here and I thought of the many kids who had stood against it when it was the outer edge of their universe, the boundary beyond which they were forbidden to pass.

An hour later I was in Len Dixon's kitchen devouring great hunks of fresh bread smothered with lashings of butter and Vegemite. His wife and daughter sat in the lounge room watching television while Dixon and I caught up. I had not seen him for nine years. In 1993 I had driven with a photographer to Smithville from Broken Hill to write a story for the *Sydney Morning Herald* about an enterprise bargaining agreement being negotiated for boundary riders. I had turned up at Dixon's home on a searing hot day. I was without a hat and he stood inside his fence and examined me intently. I noticed an aviary and asked him what kind of birds he had. 'They're finches,' Dixon said. He had around 700 birds. I asked if I could have a look and he immediately invited me in. He then took me and the photographer down to a section of the Dog Fence where recent rains had created a lake, which the Dixon family used for waterskiing. The story ran on the front page of the *Herald* and afterwards Len rang to tell me how much he had enjoyed it.

We walked down to his shed where he stores a fleet of amphibious four-wheel-drive vehicles for the rare occasions when this desiccated slab of the planet becomes submerged. Most problems, however, are caused by the desert—as fence-posts get buried under sand, tens of metres of extensions are sometimes added to keep the barrier higher than the moving dunes. 'Once I lost five miles of fence just from the force of weeds being blown up against it,' Dixon told me. 'You have got to be mad to do this job. You definitely get to like your own company.'

I drove northwards over roll after roll of dunes, heading

Len Dixon has patrolled the New South Wales Dog Fence for nearly forty years.

closer to Tilcha Gate and covering ground at a pace that was inconceivable on the South Australian track. The night before Crozier had shown me a clipping from the front page of the *Barrier Daily Truth*, dated 17 December 1959. It was a moving story about the death of two little girls just inside the Dog Fence and served as a tragic reminder of how dangerous this country can be. The story quoted from the coroner's report, which had taken evidence from the parents of three-year-old Joyce Martin and her six-year-old sister, Suzanne. Colin Martin detailed the tragedy:

I am a rabbit trapper by occupation. I was working near Tilcha Station in South Australia. On the morning of 27 November 1959, about 6.30 am, I was travelling with my wife and two children…along a private road heading towards Tilcha Homestead…I had a load of rabbits on and was taking them to the chillers at Tilcha. I was driving a 1929 Ford which I had only had about a week. The old car cut out right at Green Gully tank, about 10 miles from Tilcha Homestead and about 13 miles from my camp. I got out and had a look at the motor and…I could not get it to start. I was about a half-hour or three-quarters or more trying to fix it. It could have been longer, we didn't have a watch with us. We had no water with us at the time. I thought it best to walk back to my camp to pick up my Land Rover and bring some water back…I took my wife and children up to a tree to get shade and told them to wait there until I got back. My wife said it might be best for her to come with me because one of us might not make it as we were very thirsty then. We were going to take the children with us, but thought it best to leave them under the shade of the tree as they would not get so thirsty that way. My wife thought if one of us could not make it back the other would and get water back to the children. We only thought we would be away about four hours…

We decided to cut across country back to the camp

as it would cut a lot of miles off. After walking for about seven miles we began to feel very sick. My wife had the dry spews and pains in the stomach and I did not think I would make it back to camp. I started to chew tobacco to put moisture in my mouth. I said to my wife that if she could make it back to the road, I might make it to camp and pick her up on the way back. My wife left me there and headed back to the roadway. I started to walk on to the camp and became very exhausted. I got that thirsty I started to dig for water in a creek that I managed to come to. I dug down as far as my shoulder, but only found wet sand...I struck a road and I knew that I was about eight miles from the camp. I must have got lost before and lost my bearings. I then kept on the road all the way through until dark. Sometimes I would get ten yards and sometimes I would get a hundred yards before I would fall over. I found cows piddle on the road, it was only mud, I would lay in it to try and cool me down. I even washed my mouth out with my own piddle to get some moisture. I was about a mile off the camp when it got dark, then the clouds came over and I couldn't see the stars. I waited and the saucepan stars came out and I headed where I reckoned the camp was from there. I saw another star which I thought was in the west and I headed in that direction and must have got lost again. I wandered around and found the creek again. I saw the

Southern Cross stars in the south and started to crawl that way. I don't remember anything after that until daybreak when I heard cattle bellowing. I saw the cattle and knew they were going to water. I managed to get over onto their tracks and followed them. I only had my underpants on, I must have thrown the rest of my clothes away. I followed the cattle into water and went into it. I then crawled around to my camp which was on the other side of the water. I crawled over to the tent and had a drink of orange cordial and it made me sick. I must have blacked out then. The next thing I knew my wife woke me up. We must have been at the camp the best part of two hours before I could get on my feet again and head back for the kiddies. The clock had stopped so I couldn't say what time it was. I got the Land Rover started and we headed off. We got near to where we left the kiddies and Shirley saw a piece of their clothing. Shirley started to cry and said to go and get Bernie and them. I got back to the chillers about midday and told them what had happened.

Both girls died under marpoo trees. Another rabbiter involved in the search, Francis Andrews, said that he found:

the little girl lying under a clump of trees. She was lying on her left side almost on her chest, she only had a pair of pants on. I thought the child was asleep. I walked over

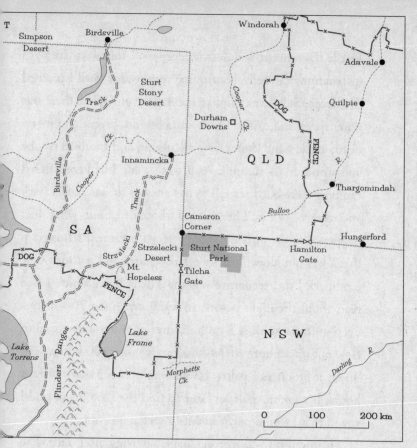

The New South Wales Dog Fence.

to her put my hand on her shoulder and said, 'Come on sweetheart', and that's when I knew she was dead. She was a very tan colour.

As I drove I thought of the Martin girls and how quickly this landscape can devour you. I reached Tilcha Gate and once through was again on Quinyambie Station in South Australia.

Inside the fence it is desert wilderness. I followed Crozier's instructions carefully, continuing southwards until I reached the Green Gully tank. Unlike the day the girls died, there was water there, and cattle. There was a hot dry breeze and it was nearly dusk. Sand dunes were all around and I walked to one and stood on its summit. As it was so late I had considered camping there but I started to feel anxious. It was such a stark and creepy place. The more I thought about what had happened to the girls the more jittery I became. I felt certain that I was not alone. I drove off in a hurry and got lost. One landmark I did recognise was the Tilcha bore, which I had read about the night before. In 1919, when the 700-metre-deep well was sunk, 4.5 million litres of water a day used to flow out into a bore stream that ran for over 100 kilometres. Today it produces a paltry 1.3 million litres every twenty-four hours. It took me half an hour to find the Dog Fence and I vowed that I would not stop until I was near people.

I drove on to Cameron Corner, arriving after dark. The modern form of the fence originated here, in Corner Country, so called because it abuts the boundaries of Queensland, New South Wales and South Australia. I found the pub, had a quick drink at the bar and drove to the empty camping ground, passing through three states on the way. I cooked rissoles and potatoes before collapsing into bed.

Vermin-proof fences were initially built along the South Australia–New South Wales border and the Queensland–New

South Wales border to halt the spread of rabbits. The SA–NSW fence ran for 584 kilometres from the Murray River in the south to Cameron Corner. The Qld–NSW fence stretched 1060 kilometres, from Cameron Corner to Mungindi.

John Cameron surveyed the New South Wales–Queensland border in September 1879. Accompanying Cameron and representing Queensland was George Chale Watson. A book called *The Surveyor* details their activities:

> These gentlemen started the survey westerly on 15 September 1879, from a point on the west bank of the Warrego River. There the surveyors erected the Zero Obelisk. The first five mile chord was then produced westerly and the mile posts off-setted from this chord to the arc, and so continued until the 141st meridian was reached, a distance of 285 miles, 24.96 chains.

This bizarre precision in such an empty landscape extended to the construction of the Dog Fence in the decade after Cameron's survey. The fence was built by the Queensland government 75 links (151 metres) inside the state, possibly to ensure that the fence would be theirs—after all, at that time its purpose was to stop rabbits moving north. Back in 1893 Henry Lawson captured beautifully the failure of the fence to hold back the sea of rabbits:

> We found Hungerford and camped there for a day. The town is right on the Queensland border, and an

interprovincial rabbit-proof fence—with rabbits on both sides of it—runs across the main street. This fence is a standing joke with Australian rabbits—about the only joke they have out there, except the memory of Pasteur and poison and inoculation. It is amusing to go a little way out of town about sunset, and watch them crack Noah's ark rabbit jokes about that fence, and burrow under and play leap-frog over till they get tired.

Lawson was writing during an era of extraordinary physical division of the continent. According to fence historian John Pickard, in 1892 there were 2.7 million kilometres of fences in New South Wales with a 1990 value of $5.6 billion. After World War I the New South Wales pastoralists wanted the fence to stop dogs moving south, and it seemed the Queenslanders no longer cared.

I went up to the shop/pub/petrol station the next morning and the only person there was the owner of Cameron Corner, Bill Mitchell. Kylie Minogue was singing 'In Your Eyes' beamed in by satellite. I could see the Dog Fence just outside the window and across the road. This is the 'famous fence', the spot where many people catch their only glimpse of the structure. Cameron Corner has also become a magnet for tourists wanting a meat pie. Because they travel in convoys they usually call ahead so Mitchell can have them hot for their arrival. 'It's so different here, and the sunsets. *Mate!*'

I drove away with Mitchell standing waving at me. Within a few minutes he would again become one of the most isolated human beings anywhere on the planet. A quirk of cartography and colonial line-making were the only reasons the tourists came to eat his pies.

Ever since seeing the scorpions in the Great Victoria Desert with Bill Sandow, I was apprehensive about finding one in my sleeping bag. Grant O'Neil, the twenty-four-year-old patrolman at Toona Gate, an hour east of Cameron Corner, is the survivor of a scorpion sting. He pulled his boot on one morning and was struck on the sole of his foot. The first sensation was like red-hot steel being pressed into his flesh. It was then numb for an entire day. When the numbness faded he had the mother of all pins and needles for several hours. Telling me this story O'Neil looked me straight in the eye. 'The pins and needles were shocking—you wouldn't fucking believe it.'

O'Neil is also a rabbit shooter. His dog has a big mauled head because it was accidentally shot at point-blank with a .22 rifle. O'Neil is married with two young children. 'It's bloody hard for the kids. You don't know whether you are doing the right thing for them, but they're as social as any others.' To help raise extra money he shoots dingoes and takes the scalps to Thargomindah in Queensland where he collects a $10-per-dog bounty. On one trip he shot 180 wild dogs in three days.

This stretch of fence used to be called Little's Fence, after sheep farmer Frank Little, who ran Mount Wood Station from 1910 to 1929. He fought vociferously for the maintenance of the barrier between Cameron Corner and Hungerford, fearing that without it the cattlemen would move in on sheep country. He would be horrified to learn that today his station is in the heart of Sturt National Park, one of the most famous desert parks in New South Wales. His homestead is now occupied by a park ranger, Ingrid Witte. The impact of the fence as an ecological wall is most apparent in Sturt. The national park is immediately inside the fence and contains an unnaturally high population of kangaroos. There has been talk of returning the reserve to a better mix of wildlife by shifting the fence southwards. The cost of this, however, would be around $10 million. In a recent paper CSIRO scientist Alan Newsome argued that allowing the dingo back into parts of the western division of New South Wales could have a dramatic impact on feral pests like pigs and goats. 'As custodians of the environment we must make a choice. What do we want? On the one hand, the evidence is clear. The dingo does a lot of the pest control work for us— while we sleep—doing work that we want done.'

Once past Toona Gate I was soon crossing the vast floodplains of the Bulloo River, nearing the end of the border section of the Dog Fence. Five kilometres from where the Queensland fence starts is Hamilton Gate, home to Len and

Frances Mohr. Frances had baked a loaf of crusty bread and put together two delicious sandwiches that made me realise how badly I had been eating. Len is fifty-four and spent most of his working life on the railways; Frances is forty-nine and worked at a nursing home. If they want to do any serious shopping they drive hundreds of kilometres to Dubbo. They have four children and seven grandchildren. Len is responsible for fifty-five kilometres of the Dog Fence and patrols it twice a week. After we had eaten, Len offered to drive me to the start of the Queensland fence. He was hoping to shoot a dingo which he had seen hanging around a carcass on the other side of Hamilton Gate. After a ten-minute drive we reached the end of the New South Wales fence. I looked due north and felt a strong urge to keep going, to drive the final 2600 kilometres but there was simply no more time. It was March 2002 and I had to get back to Sydney, which meant I had to break my journey and return some months later.

We returned to Hamilton Gate and the Mohrs invited me to stay until it cooled down. Len was hoping to shoot the dingo at sunset. I told them how unsettling Green Gully dam had been and Len told me that often when he is working on the fence he hears a voice calling out to him, 'Len! Lenny!' When he looks up there is never anybody there. We sat in the lounge room while Frances did a crossword puzzle and watched a documentary about Elvis Presley. When it was over Len and I climbed on the roof and looked across the Dog

Fence at the carcass lying just inside Queensland. Len had his rifle with him. Frances came outside to have a dig at her husband. She craned her neck up at the roof where Len and I were standing. 'They're that smart they can probably see you up there and know you're trying to shoot 'em.'

'They're not as smart as me,' Len said, without taking his eyes off the carcass, which in the dusk light cast a long shadow across the red sand. 'You know, James, if they didn't have a bounty on them I wouldn't touch them.'

The dingo did not show.

CHAPTER 10

FLEGGY GOES BUSH

A drought, which had only just started to bite when I had visited Hamilton Gate in March 2002 was now, sixteen weeks later, turning into a natural disaster. I was back on the fence with western Queensland fence inspector Peter Flegg, and I felt as though a time machine had erased March, April, May and two-thirds of June. Sydney was soggy when I had flown out twenty-four hours earlier—in a few days nearly half a metre of rain had fallen at my home on the coast. In all the time I had been away, Hamilton Gate had not felt a single drop. It was as if I had never left.

For weeks whenever I called I had listened to Flegg's voice on the answering machine. His message was the most succinct I had ever heard: 'Fleggy's gone bush, you know what to do.'

Now that I'd found him Flegg suggested driving the five kilometres down to Hamilton Gate to catch up with Len Mohr.

Len was working somewhere to the west. Frances pointed towards Queensland on the other side of the Dog Fence, to where hundreds of cattle had been watering in March. The stock were now almost completely gone. 'All that's left over there is an old heifer,' Frances said. 'I watch her every day. She has a drink and she gets up to walk away to find feed but she doesn't get far and then she has to go back for another drink. Everything is dying. The kangaroos, the emus, the cows, the birds—everything. It's very sad.'

She pointed to a cow carcass which looked like the same one I had seen nearly sixteen weeks earlier. 'With the drought, Lennie has been able to shoot thirty-five dingoes over there.'

'Did he get the one he was waiting for the day I visited?' I asked.

'Yep, just after you left.'

Fleggy and I said our goodbyes and drove the fifty metres to the border. As I climbed back in the four-wheel-drive after opening and closing Hamilton Gate, Flegg spotted a golden male dingo eating the carrion Frances had been pointing at. 'Is it OK for me to shoot it here?' he asked rhetorically. 'Is it a dingo?' A beat and then he mumbled before he lifted the scope to his eye, 'Yep.'

I blocked my ears and Fleggy fired. The dog fell as if a rug had been pulled out from under its feet. We drove over to it. I got out first and the dog rolled over to look at me and

Fleggy hangs the dingo he shot near Hamilton Gate. A dead dog is always strung on the side of the fence it was killed.

made a feeble attempt to snap. Fleggy stood with one leg on either side of the animal and it tried to snap again.

'Be careful,' I called out, afraid to walk any closer.

'What of? He's dead. We'll hang it on the fence so Lennie can scalp it.'

A dingo scalp can fetch from $50 to $100, and some farmers will pay far more than this for the head of a particularly troublesome dog. Flegg picked up the body, dropped it on top of his chainsaw in the back of the ute and drove over to the closest post on the Dog Fence. With a knife he sliced between the bone and the tendon on both of the dog's hind heels. Wire was pushed through the gashes and the dog was strung up, its body almost long enough for its snout to touch the powdery red sand. It is a tradition that dingoes are hung on the side of the fence that they are killed on.

'It's a big dog,' Fleggy said. 'It's in good condition.'

I couldn't help forgetting what the fence is for and what people out there think of dingoes. 'It's so beautiful' just slipped out as I saw how magnificent a dingo in its prime can be.

Of the three states through which the Dog Fence travels, the Queensland leg is the least known—it does not appear on any tourist maps. In fact the exact route of the structure in Queensland, where it is often called the Barrier Fence, has never been surveyed. Nowhere are there hyperbolic signs flagging its existence and nowhere does it cross any prominent tourist spots, but one thing is certain, the Queenslanders built lots of vermin-proof fences.

By 1930 there were nearly 50,000 kilometres of pest-exclusion fences—over 30,000 kilometres of which were dog-proof. In 1954, after decades of parochial dingo-fence management, the system was rationalised by the state government into a single 5680-kilometre-long Barrier Fence that travelled north of Mount Isa and halfway to Townsville, at the bottom of Cape York, before plunging south to terminate at the foothills of the rainforested Bunya Mountains.

For more than thirty years the Queensland fence was longer than the entire Dog Fence that today crosses three states. Until the mid-1980s, however, it was a poorly maintained mess that was mostly *not* dog-proof. Patrolmen were infamous for spending great slabs of their day in pubs across the state, and graziers who were subsidised to look after the Dog Fence where it passed through their properties routinely used the money for holidays or things other than fencing. In 1982 after scrapbooks full of bad press the government decided to divest itself of 3000 kilometres of the fence and set to work repairing the remainder. A 750-kilometre deviation was surveyed from Windorah to Tambo and, with an injection of $3.5 million, the modern Queensland fence was born. The commonly cited figure for its length is 2600 kilometres but Jerry Stanley has measured it as being somewhere between 2530 and 2560 kilometres; his best guess is the lower figure.

Today the Queensland operation is divided into western and eastern fences. Fleggy runs the western, from near Hamilton Gate to Tambo, and Jerry Stanley runs the eastern section from Tambo to Jandowae. Stanley also has overall responsibility for the structure.

At that moment Jerry Stanley, who in reality is the 'Lord

of the Fence', was the most important person in my life—he had the power to allow me to continue my journey. I had spoken to him only three times and each conversation had been brief and intimidating. At first he told me not to even attempt to travel the Queensland leg in March as I first intended because a monsoonal trough could sweep through making the track impassable. In May we talked about possible times for my trip and I asked if he would send me a map. In my nervousness I said I had so far managed to get through the remotest and harshest landscape that the fence passes through anywhere in Australia. There was silence, then he replied, 'It's bloody rough up here, let me tell you. And remote.'

I was worried I had offended him. A few days later, however, a huge laminated map came in the mail and the fenceline had been drawn on with a black texta. It resembled the growth graph of an internet start-up company—there was a dramatic rise into northern Queensland, followed by a series of sharp slumps and smaller rises and then for nearly 500 kilometres it ran along a jagged plateau parallel to the Warrego Highway. My path would take me near the track followed by Burke and Wills in their quest to reach the Gulf of Carpentaria, and across the Matilda Highway, so named because north of the fence was where Banjo Paterson penned Australia's real national anthem, 'Waltzing Matilda'. The Australian Labor Party was born at Barcaldine—a town that sits just above the northernmost point of the Dog Fence.

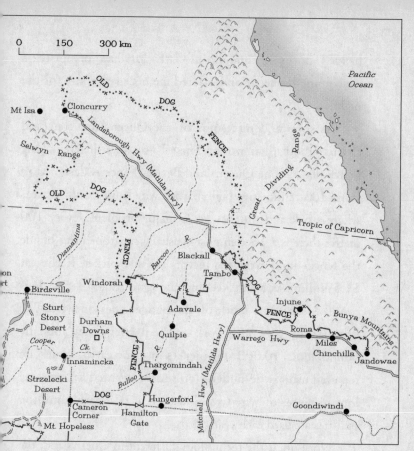

The Queensland Dog Fence.

More than anything, though, the Queensland fence would take me to communities and people that many Australians, myself included, did not know existed.

In June when I called Stanley for the third time, he referred me to Fleggy, who lives in Quilpie. I had driven from Charleville airport to Quilpie the night before Fleggy and I headed down to Hamilton Gate. He had organised a welcoming barbecue and offered me his spare room for the night.

As soon as I met some of the Queensland crew and chatted about their work I knew I was on a different Dog Fence planet. The Queensland Barrier Fence is designed to stand 183 centimetres high. Barbed wire is used only in areas where stock and dingoes are a major problem. Every 100 metres there is a wooden post—usually cut from a tree beside the fence—and every ten metres is a star picket. Each year $1.5 million is spent keeping the Queensland fence dog-proof. Nearly one tenth of the budget goes on wire. The twenty-three men who work on the Barrier Fence annually pound about 10,000 star pickets into the earth. Holes are repaired using a tie-puller—originally invented for twisting looped pieces of wire to seal hessian bags. Nearly a million pull-ties are used each year.

Not only is the technology different in Queensland, the fence is run under a different system. The Barrier Fence has two bases—Quilpie, where Fleggy's men live, and Roma, where Stanley's crew is based. The men work rotating shifts of five days and then nine. Every eighty to 100 kilometres along the fence is a bush camp equipped with an airconditioned hut, water, electricity and a barbecue. All the men on the Queensland fence are public servants and are supplied with a vehicle. They nearly always work in pairs and their equipment is the best that Jerry Stanley can procure.

At about 4.30 am Fleggy's men arrived in his yard in a sudden rush of dust and blinding headlights. Fleggy and I left town at the civilised time of 6 am, an hour after the other men headed off to begin their week's work in the desert. From Quilpie we would head to Thargomindah—the last petrol station or shop I would see for nearly 1000 kilometres.

I began to feel excited at being on the fence again. I knew that in a few days I would be back in step with the simplicity of fence time. Soon I would be in the landscape where there seemed to be no foreground or middle ground—only a great dizzying horizon.

Peter Flegg is short and stocky and forty-one years old. Before his ten years on the fence he was shooting starlings, which are agricultural pests, on the Nullarbor for the Western Australian government. He also spent three years on a farm and nearly eight as a mechanic. With his battered hat on he looks like a tough fence inspector; beneath it he has a kind and friendly face and a shock of difficult-to-control wavy hair. He walks with a bounce, is a hard worker and keen hunter, and he has sliced onion in his sandwiches almost every day. He also never puts his handbrake on when he steps out of his still-rolling car to make repairs to the fence. It is as if Fleggy has total faith in the flatness of the desert.

'The first thing I noticed when I came out here,' Fleggy told me, 'was that Jerry and his men were pretty fucking serious about the fence.' He said this without taking his eyes off the netting he was inspecting. 'Fuck me, we're having a good run today. We'll find holes but there's a difference between holes and negligence. I would be pretty disappointed if I came out here and found the fence wasn't dog-proof.'

The curse of the Queensland patrolmen is feral pigs, and between Hamilton Gate and Zenonie camp Fleggy spotted a family of three on the other side of the fence. He stopped the car and aimed his rifle at the boar, hitting it but not dropping it. Next he fired at the sow, paralysing her hindquarters. She turned as if to tear down the fence in a bloody rage. Her face showed no fear whatsoever, only hate, and for the second time that day I was afraid of a wounded wild animal. A second bullet left her twitching in the dust. The piglet had bolted along the fence and in a few seconds Fleggy's vehicle had caught up to it. A single shot killed it instantly. 'Pigs have got no respect,' Fleggy said, packing his rifle behind my seat. 'You'll never stop pigs.'

That night while I prepared dinner, he connected a high-frequency radio in my car so that I would be able to communicate with him or Jerry. Every morning Fleggy talks to all of his men, finds out where they are and what they plan to do, issues his instructions, catches up on their welfare and often shares a joke. Then Jerry comes on, talks to all his men and to Fleggy. Throughout the day everybody listens in to everyone else's conversations. The radio is a powerful tool for the inspectors, who know that every word they utter is listened to for nuance. The twenty-three staff are spread out along 2600 kilometres, so good communication is imperative for safety and for morale—it is a superb way for the bosses to let everyone know who is doing a good job, and a brutally public method of keeping slackness to a minimum.

'We got a wolf yesterday,' Fleggy broadcast to his men before moving on to the business of the day. His description of the dingo he had killed the day before took me by surprise. Australians are brought up to regard dingoes as slinking finks, unworthy of anything other than a bullet or a poison bait. The creature hanging on the fence near Hamilton Gate, however, *was* more like a wolf than a skulking dingo.

At mid-morning, on top of a rocky rise, Fleggy found three piglets huddled inside a twist of netting. One by one he pulled them out by their legs, swung them through the air in a giant loop and killed them instantly by smashing their heads on the edge of a boulder. At lunchtime we reached a rise that looked down across the Bulloo River floodplains, where the only way to inspect the fence was on foot. Fleggy would stop and repair the fence by placing sawn logs onto the bottom of the wire to hold the fold of netting on the ground in place. For several hundred metres the Dog Fence travels on top of a dramatic clifftop karst system comprising dozens of caves of various sizes, with bird nests and mummified wallaby carcasses inside. We descended towards the Bulloo River, the first waterway I had come to in 3500 kilometres that had water in it.

We headed straight to Peter 'Blue' Maher's homestead on the Bulloo but there was no one home. Fleggy and I waited for two hours, listening to the windmill creak and watching the pelicans, swans and herons cruising on the muddy waters. We drove on to the Barrier Fence camp known as Dino's Cave—two patrolmen built a wooden dinosaur skeleton outside the camp which has since become a minor tourist attraction. It was a beautiful spot, surrounded by gidgee scrub. Power comes from a diesel-fuelled generator and water is heated by a wood-fired construction called a donkey. The shower is underneath the tank stand, which has a pipe flowing into a 40-gallon drum, situated on top of a fireplace. Water pressure forces the hot water through a dinner-plate-sized shower rose. The contraption was very important to me because the dust was driving me crazy and a daily shower had fast become my greatest physical pleasure.

Most of the rest of the day we drove through a fog of brown dust out of which kangaroos and emus emerged like ghosts. We came across a big male red kangaroo that was so injured or feeble it could not move. Flegg climbed out, walked up to the roo and shot it point-blank. The blast popped the marsupial's eyes right out of its head. 'Fuck it,' Flegg said, 'I've got my tinnitus back.'

All day, however, my thoughts had been about one thing

only: that night I would be meeting with Jerry Stanley, and as our rendezvous got closer I was getting more anxious. It seemed as if everyone had a story about forty-five-year-old Stanley.

Dinah Percival, author of *Fence People*, met Stanley when he was twenty-nine. 'He's outspoken, flamboyant and, according to his father, "a bad-tempered bugger. Terrible bloody boy."'

Author Phillip Holden met Jerry three years after Percival. 'The man himself greeted me at the door. He was a big, hulking character sporting a Mexican-bandit moustache. Still in his work clothes. Like me, he was in dire need of a shower. He gave me a bear-like paw to shake, introduced me to his wife, Marie, and started for the door.'

The pair then went to the pub and drank until Holden staggered off to bed. Jerry kicked on until 3 am at a friend's place and was ready for work a few hours later as bright as a button. Holden was so hungover he could barely function.

I wasn't sure what to expect. Bill Sandow had told me to make sure I got drunk with Stanley. I have had to deal with a lot of tough guys in my work as a journalist and have never yet met one that wasn't soft underneath. Perhaps because I am not a tall man big blokes enjoy slapping me on the back and throwing an arm around my shoulder. I have also learnt that with hard men you have to be hard back. Feeling confident now, I told Fleggy that I wouldn't be surprised if Jerry, too, turned out to be a marshmallow. Fleggy sucked in air and then chuckled. 'He would tear you limb from limb if he heard you call him a marshmallow.'

For the past three days I had been listening to radio chatter where the main topic of conversation was dust. Jerry and his men were helping the 'western fellas' with fence reconstruction in the Wilson River overflow, and men who had worked for many years on the Barrier Fence had never before experienced dust the likes of which they were now battling. Camp 16 was the name of the donga, or workman's hut, where we would be meeting, and as we drove in Fleggy radioed me to slow down to avoid dumping dust on the men enjoying a dusk beer. Even so a mini cloud floated behind me when I came to a halt and I could see four or five pairs of eyes watching to see whether I was a high or medium-level city wanker. I took one look at Jerry who sat coolly on the verandah and hoped that he and I were going to get on. He didn't stand up to greet me and his expression didn't change.

The sun was going down, all the men had finished work and were filthy with dust as if they had fallen into a barrel of wholemeal flour. Beers were out in coolers and dinner condiments were on the table. Most importantly, it was the State of Origin rugby night—the final of the series no less. State of Origin is an annual ritual between Queensland and New South Wales rugby league players. I was a lone Sydneysider amid half a dozen seriously rugged maroons. As any of my friends will attest, however, I have never watched an entire game of football on television or listened to a match on the radio. In the middle of a desert wilderness the radio was all we had. I did not have a clue who won the series the season before but that night I would be New South Wales' number one fan.

There were still a couple of hours before the game began and Stanley started to quiz me on what I had seen, how the other states ran their sections, what problems I had encountered and what I thought of the Queensland barrier so far. I liked him and, when he wasn't around, his men spoke glowingly of Stanley's memory, his endurance, his practical skills, his fighting prowess and his unbureaucratic ways. I saw that he had an intensity about everything that he did. For the first hour I was with him I felt as though I was standing in rough surf trying to stay on my feet. His men told me later that he suffers terribly from insomnia, often lying awake for hours worrying about some minor detail of the fence. When he does sleep, the patrolmen, who all roll out their swags around him, often have to listen to his complicated monologues. More than one patrolman told me that he has even held conversations with Jerry about the fence while he was asleep.

Many beers were drunk and I sealed my acceptance with the crew by being able to tell them the game was starting a half-hour earlier than normal because of a World Cup soccer

Camp 16. From left to right: Peter Flegg, Darryl Barwick, Robert Black, Jerry Stanley.

semi-final, also being played that night. The teams tied but Queensland got to keep the gong because, as I learned from Robert Black, Stanley's right-hand man in the east, in the event of a draw the trophy stayed with the previous year's winners.

I slept in my car. Jerry was in his swag and was still talking. He was saying something about huge flocks of emus. He didn't slow down. Instead his voice suddenly stopped until about 5.30 am, when the first sound heard was Jerry again, launching us into a new day.

It is hard to believe that Stanley is a public servant, and one of the conditions he insisted on when he took on the job was to do things his way—a 2600-kilometre fence across the outback cannot be maintained by a man hamstrung by red tape. The fence requires numerous compromises with graziers, little deals, and staff that cannot afford to be clock watchers. When you work for the Barrier Fence you work for Jerry Stanley and you work by his rules. During my first week of training in the navy a small group of us was called to a 'meeting' after senior cadets learned that an admiral would be visiting us to find out if we were being bastardised. We were told to keep our mouths shut. 'This is not a democracy!' one of the seniors had screamed at us. I could imagine Jerry likewise warning his men, 'This is not a bureaucracy!'

CHAPTER 11

NOTHING IS AN EXAGGERATION

In the pre-dawn Stanley's biggest worry was the dust. 'You better sool yer boys out,' he said to Blacky. 'The air's so still there'll be that much dust it will take them an hour to get out to the fence.' The fence was only a few kilometres away so I was sure that Stanley was exaggerating.

He told me to follow him but as soon as he left the compound it was impossible to see where his car was. I could not see even a metre beyond the bonnet. I slowed down and aimed for the thickest part of the cloud. Dust hung in the air like a fog. I grabbed my notebook and, without being able to see the page, scrawled a note: NOTHING IS AN EXAGGERATION.

I suddenly found myself outside the cloud into a clear dawn sky and knew I had made a wrong turn. I reversed back into the tunnel of dust and after fifteen minutes thought I saw brakelights ahead. I stopped. Jerry opened the door. 'We've been trying to call you on the radio. Did you hear us?'

'No, I haven't turned the radio on yet,' I replied lamely.

'Whenever you're in the car you *must* have the radio on. It's not just for your safety either. Someone may be in trouble and be trying to call. Don't forget to turn it on.'

Jerry's plan for me was that over the next week I should get myself to the end of the western division. He would then take me through to Roma, 600 kilometres from the end of the fence. Before I drove off, Stanley told me to contact two people before we next met—the mayor of Quilpie, Dave Edwards, and a Windorah pastoralist, Sandy Kidd. I always like to know a little bit about anyone I am advised to speak to, so I asked why they were important. Stanley looked into my eyes. 'Jim, you talk to them and find out for yourself. I'm just telling ya that you've got to talk to them.' I knew I needed to get my Dog Fence passport stamped with those two names before Stanley would let me continue my journey.

Soon I was on my own for the first time in days and chewing on no one's dust. Jerry had told me that a few kilometres beyond the reconstruction work was a clearing with so many kangaroos on it that when they are disturbed 'it looks as though the plain got up and walked away'. It was true—the grassy area, hundreds of hectares, was seething with red kangaroos. As they fled from the noise of the car, lines of the silhouetted marsupials bounded away at 40 kilometres per hour; it was as if the landscape inside the fence had black waves travelling across it. Emus were on the plain as well and I imagined what it would be like to see the huge flocks of running birds Jerry had described the night before.

The morning passed quickly. I was driving across a treeless moonscape, reminiscent of Coober Pedy. Every few hundred metres wedge-tailed eagles sat on the fenceposts, only lifting themselves lazily off their vantage points when I got within a few metres. Mobs of kangaroos skipped along in front of me, kicking up puffs of dust with every leap. In the middle of the day I saw a young joey flicked out of its mother's pouch to land in front of the car. Its mother and the mob bounded away. I stopped and got out of the car but I didn't know what to do. The joey wasn't even knee-height and it was disoriented and frightened. I felt sure that the mother would come back, but was concerned that an eagle might spot him. But I couldn't take the joey with me. I still had 2000 kilometres to travel. I kept going, hoping the creature would be OK.

On a long stretch of floodplain I caught up to patrolmen Paul Gray and Terry White. Gray is a big Viking-like character, with blond hair and a goatee. White is handsome and quiet. I had met both men in the pre-dawn dark at Quilpie before my trip with Fleggy. Gray sensed that I was in a hurry and pulled me up about it. 'What are you trying to do?' he asked. 'Drive across Australia in eight days? You should

Jerry Stanley, aka 'Lord of the Fence'.

slow down and look more closely at the fence. If you go too fast you'll miss too much.'

I said goodbye and moved on but, after struggling with a booby-trap-like cocky gate that cracked me in the ribs, I felt so exhausted I could have lain down in the dirt and slept. I decided, in spite of my promise to meet Stanley in a few days' time, to heed Gray's warning and slow down. I decided to stop at Raymore camp and radioed back to Gray. He gave me directions and said they would arrive half an hour after me.

Gray looks after 400 kilometres of fence and there are four or five dongas along his run alone. 'They're not just a bunk,' he told me. 'They have got to be part of our life.' The Raymore donga is located behind a windmill-filled dam. It has the standard deep-green verandah and a high tin roof is held in place by four tree-trunks painted white. Inside the decor is a combination of 'caravan' and $40-a-night motel room. It was spotless and had everything that a patrolman could want—a flushing toilet, hot water, a fridge stocked with beer and food, a good stove and a cupboard full of girlie magazines. On one wall was a poster of a centrefold girl named Belinda. She was almost life-size and, after a day of driving through gritty dust, her glossy, naked body looked other-worldly. Gray and White arrived and from the back of their ute pulled out a chamois container with a goanna in it. It was a black-headed monitor (*Varanus tristis*), and its back was as intricately decorated as if it were a living Aboriginal dot painting. They had caught it to show me as an example of the beautiful things to see out on the fence.

Paul Gray and I started talking. He has been on the fence for three years and has worked as a kangaroo shooter and skinner. 'Nobody's here for the money,' he began. 'I'm not on any flash cash. I bring home $1154 a fortnight. I don't want the job for the money, I want it because of what I can enjoy and get out of the environment.'

Gray stood up to get himself another beer. 'We're driving around following something that's only about two inches wide. Why are we doing it?' He sounded genuinely baffled. 'What it's designed to keep out—dingoes—does the least damage to it. A dog might slip in through an old kangaroo or pig hole but it doesn't do anywhere near the damage caused by other animals like pigs.' He paused for a moment.

'You can tell a lot about the people before you on the fence, you can tell whether they were lazy or whether they had a bit of pride in their work. The fence tells a story every week that we come out here. There's only two erasers out here— rain and wind. Without them your tracks and the tracks of everybody else can lie out here for months. You can tell the movements of animals weekly, you can see where a cocky has been out to the fence to check on your work. In some places I can see tracks where I drove six months ago. It's a little story-book in itself. You can put together some pretty interesting things, some detailed stories.'

In the morning Gray described the landmarks the fence passes through to Cooper Creek and ended with the command, 'No matter what, don't miss the waterhole.' He was talking about Munamerrie waterhole.

For nearly 1000 kilometres I felt as though I had seen nothing but death, starvation, suffering and dust. At Munamerrie I arrived at an antipodean oasis. Pelicans in huge

Terry White and Paul Gray. 'Our job is to maintain the fence.'

numbers sailed across the sky. Three brolgas honked and danced. Coolibah trees, which looked as though they had seen and shrugged off a thousand droughts, draped off the river-bank, their root systems the size of suburban backyards. I craned my neck to watch as an enormous flock of pelicans came in to land like sea planes and disturbed swarms of finches and parrots. There must be many such places near the Dog Fence that I had driven past in my ignorance. The fence may be a primitive wildlife management tool, the ecological equivalent of a caveman's club, but just out of view are places that humans have hardly touched.

The fence is linear thinking taken to an extreme degree but I realised that it was a different world, one all of its own. In South Australia and New South Wales I had been in such depopulated environments that I was forced to travel both sides of the fence to find humans. It would be possible to travel from the Great Australian Bight to the New South Wales border dozens of times and never see more than a handful of people on the wire. In Queensland the fence was home for twenty-three men and it felt like a large number of people.

I stopped at a telephone booth in Windorah and called Sandy Kidd as Jerry Stanley had instructed. He was home and I drove straight over. Kidd, while much older than Jerry, is cut from the same slab of coolibah—passionate, practical, in tune with his land and a fierce defender of the fence, 1080 poisoning and the fabled oasis of Cooper Creek. 'You have got to have a line in the sand to control pests,' he told me. 'Don't you worry, they'll go for anything from a pig to a calf. I have seen up to twenty-four dingoes pull a beast down. They'll work a mob of cattle until the calf falls back to the tail of the mob.'

All of his life Kidd has been an active man in outback Queensland, involved in agricultural politics, lobbying for the fence and the eradication of dingoes. In the late 1990s he shot to national prominence as the ringleader of the local pastoralists who ran the cotton irrigators, with their modern surveying laser levellers and poisons, out of town. For the last eight months, because of the drought, he had been selling his stock. His father had drummed into Sandy a rule of thumb: 'If you can't see the feed in front of the stock sell them. It's better to sell them than smell them.'

We talked over an hour and then he took me outside to see, of all things, a pet dingo called Kenny. Kidd cautioned me not to expect too much from Kenny in the way of friendliness. Typical of most captive dingoes, even though he'd been caught as a pup, he is friendly with only a couple of people. He especially loves Kidd's grand-daughter, Holly. 'I have chased dingoes all my life but I respect their brains,' Kidd said.

Before I left he showed me an old family photograph that featured Harry Redford—the cattle rustler better known as Captain Starlight, immortalised in the classic Australian novel *Robbery under Arms*. In 1870 Redford took a stolen mob of 400 cattle from central Queensland to South Australia through country that had consumed Burke and Wills a decade earlier.

Gray and White caught up with me in Windorah later that afternoon. 'I've got something for you,' Gray said, rummaging around in his ute. He handed me a chunk of fencepost from the Dog Fence which he had cut off with his chainsaw. The top was so weathered after 100 years of exposure it was spiky and the colour of elephant hide. The wood inside, however, was still as red as it would have been when the tree it came from was felled. After a century of punishment from the sun with temperatures exceeding 50 degrees Celsius, dust storms, rain and white ants, the wood had nothing more than a fetching grey suntan.

A hand-drilled hole in the top had two pieces of wire threaded through. 'Even that wire tells a story,' Gray said to me. 'Do you know why?'

I looked at it carefully. 'This is the old original wire and that is the new galvanised wire,' I replied.

He gave me a nod that said I was learning my lessons well.

That night over dinner Gray and White drank the best part of a case of beer between them and surprised me with the gift of a six-pack of bourbon and cola. We then went to the pub and played darts with a group of strangers.

'I bet you it's the longest time machine in the world,' Gray reflected about the fence. 'There are heaps of objects along it from the past—bottles, tyres, machinery parts, old buttons. At some of the old homesteads near the fence you find cutlery, pots and plates. From well back in the fifties there are the old camps of the patrolmen who passed through.'

White left before the game was over and when Gray and I returned home he was asleep, fully clothed on top of his swag. The pair reminded me of two hard-working shepherds with extraordinary camaraderie. All the Dog Fence patrolmen are the same—Stanley and Fleggy go to enormous lengths to ensure that each man is paired with a good fit. The patrolmen are paid nearly $50 a night as a swag allowance and must sleep at their camps, which means that Stanley's men spend more time with their work partners than they do with their own families.

I woke before dawn to a frosty, cold morning. That day I had several hundred kilometres of fence to cover. In order to continue on to Tambo, however, I would need to leave the maintenance track at the end of the day and drive 100 kilometres back to Quilpie. There I would refuel and meet the mayor, Dave Edwards, before returning to the fence to continue my journey.

Outside Windorah on Hammond Downs Station the fence branches off in two directions. This is what Queenslanders call 'the deviation'—the starting point where nearly 3000 kilometres of Dog Fence was removed from the Queensland government's books in the early 1980s. The old fence was still in place, but within metres of the fork there were holes in the marsupial netting. Posts were bent over and supported only by the residual tension of a few bits of rusted wire.

Gravity cannot be seen but an abandoned Dog Fence is like a sheet thrown over the invisible man and at once gravity has a form. We are all pressed downwards. Earth wants us all to lie down flat upon her skin. The old redundant fence reminded me of one of the ghost fishing nets that environmentalists complain about—drift nets cut loose, floating across the ocean trapping fish. I was sure an interesting adventure lay along this abandoned front line, but my path was beside the fence without holes.

Everywhere around me was evidence of drought. Only trees and large shrubs were left standing—all grass was gone, and every animal I saw was sickly and weak. Back in February the emus on the South Australian fence ran for kilometres without showing a trace of fatigue. The animals I was passing near Windorah were dying. I was no longer afraid to overtake emus as they ran along the fence but I felt guilty knowing they were expending their last reserves to escape me. The most pathetic sight was the countless emus who had lost their powerful, fluid gait, and now ran as unsteadily as a day-old foal. They would all die on the fence.

CHAPTER 12
DEVIL'S GATES

After a hard-learned lesson some years ago I now live by a friend's motto, 'lose your head and you lose your hat', yet all day my mind failed to focus on the job at hand. Instead I had been preoccupied with a problem in Sydney. I was, however, home and hosed. That night, 29 June, I would camp with Fleggy and meet the mayor of Quilpie at a party held by the town's polocrosse club after a day of competition. I was close to the road where I would leave the fence and head to Adavale and Quilpie so I decided to pull over and have a snack. I drove into an area which had been freshly bulldozed and started to eat when I heard a sickening sound: ttttssss, ttttssss, ttttssss. At first the noise came rhythmically, like a train puffing, then I realised it was in stereo.

'Fleggy, are you there, mate?' I called into the HF radio trying to keep my voice sounding calm, hoping that the inspector was at home.

'Got you, Woody,' he replied.

'Mate, I have a problem. I've two flat tyres and only one spare.'

'Stand by, Woody,' he said. 'I'll make a few calls to Adavale and see if somebody might be able to come out and get you.' A few minutes later he was back on the radio. 'Foetal and I are on the way.'

Not since the dawn I shared with Bill Sandow back in the Great Victoria Desert had the idea of a travelling the Dog Fence seemed such a stupid self-indulgent idea. It was a Saturday afternoon, my wife was back in Sydney working, my three children were missing me, we had $200 left in our bank account, and I was fumbling with a jack for an expensive four-wheel-drive in the middle of a drought-stricken desert. Worst of all, two men I hardly knew were driving 150 kilometres to help me. Second worst of all, two dozen men listening to the radio would have heard in my voice that I was barely holding it together. Confirming my fears, Paul Gray's voice came over the radio, reminding Fleggy to bring the right wheel size for my vehicle.

Within an hour a plume of dust appeared in the distance and Flegg and his colleague, Peter 'Foetal' Shultz, climbed out. I had met Foetal twice since arriving at Quilpie—the first time at the barbecue Fleggy organised, the second at the Wilson overflow. He had short brown hair and buckets of street cunning. It was clear that he was a fast talker. He was also one of the youngest men on the fence and Stanley rode him hard.

Soon we had changed both tyres. I told them how sorry I was for ruining their afternoon. 'Don't worry, Woody, we were only watching *Shrek* for the third or fourth time,' Fleggy said. He would have been offended at the big hug I felt like giving him and instead I promised the best token of gratitude that one man in the outback can give to another—a slab of cold beer. Yet if it wasn't for the breakdown I would have missed one of those subtleties of the fence that Paul Gray encouraged me to see. This time it was the name of the spot—Give and Take Corner. The fence had a deliberate kink in it, like a badly set broken limb, to help a neighbouring pastoralist access a precious creek. It seemed like the most appropriate place along 5400 kilometres of wire that I could have broken down.

We were back in Quilpie by 6 pm. Foetal cooked a meal, which included onion, chicken fillets, sliced sausage, tomatoes, apple puree, tinned peas, Tabasco sauce, a handful of salt and soup mix. We watched television until Fleggy fell asleep. As Foetal and I crept out of Fleggy's house, I felt like a teenager breaking curfew for an illicit night on the tiles.

We walked to the party and I spent over an hour talking to Dave Edwards about his town, his farm, and the drought. It was, he said, the worst in white man's history. He and his sons were now pulling mulga forests down to provide last-resort fodder for their sheep.

Edwards grew up on a property at Thargomindah with

the Barrier Fence flanking three sides. On three occasions his father had to sell all of his sheep because dingoes were in such high numbers. 'Sometimes,' he told me, 'the dogs were so bad that sheep kept in yards less than 100 metres from the homestead would be mauled. It was nothing to come out and find fifteen sheep killed by dingoes.' Eventually his father moved deep inside the fence to Quilpie to get away from the dogs. 'I have always had an interest in the dog problem and the fence. We need to keep the Barrier Fence because sheep are a great boost every year to our local economy.'

Edwards had recently been made chair of the Barrier Fence Board. He has been involved in local politics as an independent candidate since 1969 and been mayor of Quilpie since 1997. He is also one of Jerry's biggest admirers and has known him for more than twenty-five years. 'The fence is probably the best it's ever been. It's like everything, it's the man at the helm that's the main contributor, and Jerry's good.'

The next morning was memorable for several reasons. I showered in Quilpie's bore water. It turned my silver wedding band a fluorescent blue-black colour. A biochemist later told me that the transformation was caused by the same process that gave birth to photography. As I marvelled at my ring and wondered whether it would ever return to normal, I watched Fleggy fix my two flat tyres. It made me realise what a gulf there was between a man like me and a gifted practical person such as Fleggy. My father left home when I was six years old and I never learned how to make or fix things like my friends who had been shown by their dads. For the rest of my journey I would hear Fleggy make his daily scheduled radio calls but I would not see him again and I wasn't sure how to thank him. He seemed embarrassed when I tried.

On the way into Quilpie the night before, I had seen what looked like an injured emu. In broad daylight, driving away, I saw the bird again. It was seriously hurt, with one leg flopping loosely below a compound fracture. I climbed out of the car and found a log. The bird tried to run but couldn't. I stood in front of it, swung the wood, aiming for the side of its head. The blow would have only contributed to the emu's suffering. I swung again and the wood hit its head so hard that it split my knuckle.

It seemed a bad omen. I felt constricted and uncomfortable and had an intuition that all was not well. Past Adavale, a few minutes later, I was back on the Dog Fence. Within 200 metres I had another flat tyre. I had one spare and it was now in use. Should I go back to Quilpie, like a man who never wanted to leave, or gamble and drive to Tambo? I drove on. Throughout that morning I kept hearing a hissing sound but every time I stopped to check all I discovered was that my imagination was working overtime.

My destination that night was Boondoon hut, also

known as Ned's camp because Paul Gray had built a Ned Kelly statue out of tin there. The artwork helps give each of the dongas its own personality and is a way for the men to pass the long hours they spend at the camps after a day patrolling. I arrived at Boondoon just after sunset, and understood why more than one unwitting visitor arriving in the dark had got a shock when they first saw Ned with his rifle.

I lit a fire and barbecued a great mound of sausages, eggs, bacon and potato and fell asleep. At 5 am I rose, and it was so cold that to warm the dongas I resorted to a trick I had seen the patrolmen employ—I lit the stovetop burners. The water in the pipes was frozen and none of the taps worked. Even the place where I had spat out my toothpaste was marked by a blue-white mound of ice. I left early to enjoy the warmth of the car's heater.

As I drove along, emu numbers kept increasing until there were dozens in front of me. Small flocks coalesced into bigger ones like raindrops on a windscreen. Soon there were at least 500 emus in front of me pounding along the track. It was a breathtaking sight that made me swear and whistle to myself; it was also an unnatural phenomenon. The combination of the drought and the fence had created this doomed mob desperate to reach water and feed. At the top of a rise I could see a right-angle turn in the fence. When the birds reached the corner they kept going straight ahead, crashing through the brigalow scrub. As the last stragglers vanished

Boondoon hut, also known as Ned's camp. Sculpture by patrolman Paul Gray.

into the bush, I stopped the car and pinched myself to check whether what I had seen was real.

Half an hour later I met up with Skeeta who has worked the fence for thirteen years and whose voice I knew well from the daily calls to Jerry Stanley. I told him about the emus and he too had noticed big mobs building up.

The maintenance track along the fence to Tambo regularly switched sides. There were no signs to indicate which side I needed to be driving on or which gates I should go through, but Skeeta told me what he teaches all newcomers to the fence. Look at which side the pull-ties used to repair the fence are facing, because that is nearly always the side the patrolman drives along. The name of the station is written on gates to be driven through. Armed with this information I was confident that I would make Tambo that afternoon. On the way I killed three more injured emus and a wallaby. The marsupial had some kind of spinal injury and it was unable to hop away from me, instead jumping in palsied leaps.

I passed a double gate in the Dog Fence decorated spectacularly with two devils, complete with horns and tridents. Farmhouses were nearby and for the first time in 4500 kilometres I was travelling through a rural area rather than an arid wilderness. I was depressed at the evidence of landclearing—in places the only trees left standing were the monster bottle trees, whose vast girths reminded me of the baobab trees of the Kimberley.

Soon after the Devil's Gates the car started to make a strange sound. Wire stuck around the drive shaft? The suspension stuffed? Something loose? I stopped and clambered under the car. Nothing. The noise got steadily worse. I radioed Skeeta. 'Mate, how far is it from the Devil's Gates to the highway?' I asked, trying to give no indication that anything was wrong. I was so afraid of missing my meeting with Jerry Stanley that, instead of stopping at one of the homesteads, I kept driving. Lose your head and you lose your hat. Somehow I nursed the car across twenty horrendously rough kilometres and then, with the highway almost in sight, I knew I could go no further without help. 'Jerry, are you there, mate? It's James here.'

'Go ahead, James, it's Jerry.'

'Jerry, the car is making a terrible knocking noise. I think it might be the suspension.'

'Sounds like loose wheel nuts to me,' he said instantly.

'I've already checked that.'

Fleggy piped in from the western extreme of outback Queensland that it sounded like something was wrong with the suspension. I told them I would check again. I walked around the car. The nuts on one wheel had come loose, tearing the hub apart. Only three nuts were left. I thought of the two dozen sets of ears about to hear my call to Stanley. 'You're right, Jerry. The wheel nuts have come off.'

The car limped the last few kilometres to the highway and then stopped. Back on a public road I retreated to the privacy of a satellite phone I had borrowed to call the company from whom I hired the vehicle. I was exactly half-way between two of the most isolated towns in western Queensland—Blackall and Tambo. Quite amazingly, considering the outback murder of Peter Falconio a year earlier, everybody who passed and saw my hazard and interior lights on stopped to ask if I was OK. Even a mother with three young children pulled over. Eventually, sick of explaining myself to hospitable Queenslanders, I turned off the lights and waited for the tow-truck driver.

The damage looked as though it was going to be *really expensive*. How was I going to meet Jerry in Roma? I rang him on the sat phone and suggested that we meet in Tambo instead. Finally there were no more calls to be made. I looked skyward and saw how the Milky Way appears when there are no trees to block the view of the horizon; when there is no moon, no pollution and no streetlight. In the Great Victoria Desert there had been stupendous stars but, because of the wind, Sandow camped in hollows between sand dunes or within stands of trees. On the Landsborough Highway I saw that our galaxy is not a straight splash across the sky but is curved rather like a banana and is utterly vast and beautiful. If I hadn't encountered car trouble I would never have seen that view and it was all that I could cling to for comfort, knowing that the repair bill was going to hit me harder than the lever of a highly strung cocky gate.

Brett Whitfield turned up with his truck and trailer and with him came a light that banished the glow of the universe. He also phoned ahead to ensure that a toasted sandwich would be ready for me when I arrived in Blackall. I booked into a $15-a-night room in a pub. I would have to leave my car in town so it could be repaired and then hitchhike 100 kilometres south to Tambo to meet Stanley at 9 the next morning. I set my alarm for 4.30 am and slept. I had a terrible dream that a giant, disfiguring cancer grew on my face. My eyes were on the end of putrid black stalks and my flesh smelt like rotting roadkill. I woke up at 4 am crying. As I dragged my load of gear to the roadhouse to begin hitching, I could only attribute my dream to Fleggy's execution of the injured kangaroo, whose eyes had popped out of their sockets.

It was cold and Blackall was asleep. I approached a road-train driver who was stirring in his cabin and asked if I could get a lift to Tambo. He was sympathetic but not heading that way until the end of the day.

Several trucks came and passed but none stopped. If I didn't have a lift by 8 am I would have to call Jerry and get him to pick me up. At 7.45 a taciturn road-train driver pulled in. 'Any chance of a lift, mate?' I asked.

'I 'spose,' he replied, 'but not for a while. I'm going to have breakfast first.'

The silver nomads were now moving and filling up. No one could give me a ride. Just when all seemed lost a minivan pulled up and an elderly man with a great big smile offered me a lift. 'Are you in a hurry though?' he asked. 'Pity,' he said to my reply. 'I'm walking from Darwin to Melbourne and I need someone to follow me in my car.' The penny dropped. This was a guy I had heard on the radio a week earlier, who had received a vision from God to raise money for his church in Darwin. Unfortunately my time was up.

I rang Jerry from the phone booth. He told me to jump in with the truck driver after his breakfast and to get out to where I had broken down the night before. At that moment a shining silver sedan towing an immaculate caravan pulled in. This time I was desperate. 'I'm late for a meeting with a very important man,' I pitched to the startled driver as he removed his petrol cap. 'I need a ride fifty kilometres down the road and I promise to tell you a great story.'

'I don't normally pick up hitchhikers. What do you think, Lorraine?'

She nodded. Holidaymakers Terry and Lorraine Molden were heading back home to north-west Tasmania. I told them about the Dog Fence. They had no idea that it travelled so far or that it crossed the highway between Blackall and Tambo. Terry was curious about the fence, my trip and Jerry Stanley. I had promised them a story and they got one. Time was once again moving at its proper pace.

At 8.45 I saw Jerry's car by the Dog Fence. The driver's door was open and, with his knees slightly bent so that the middle of his broad back was pressed against the edge of the door, Stanley was moving side to side and up and down. His face was blank with pleasure. He was scratching himself like a bull would against a post or a tree. He was wearing his big black hat and his jeans. I had told the Moldens that Stanley is the Dog Fence personified and they were so curious to meet him that Terry jumped straight out of the car to shake his hand. 'I've got a stray for you,' he said.

I climbed into Stanley's car as the Moldens drove off and

began to fasten my seat belt. 'Don't waste your time,' Stanley said, without even looking at me. 'There's no point putting your belt on. This is the home of the gates.'

He was telling the truth. Exactly 914 fences cross the maintenance track beside the Queensland Dog Fence. Each one has a gate and, because the graziers know that the only people who pass through are patrolmen, they are invariably cocky gates, which cost next to nothing to install.

Stanley was in excellent spirits. 'This is hard, rugged, isolated, perishable country.' He gestured to the land around him. 'This all goes under water.' Ten minutes later. 'This all goes under water.' A few minutes later still. 'This all goes under water.' We were in the Barcoo River overflow country—here the Barcoo and the Thompson meet to form Cooper Creek. 'We rebuild, renew or reconstruct 120 to 150 kilometres of the Barrier Fence every year—twelve grand per kilometre for the luxury version and normally seven to eight grand. This all goes under water. It's beautiful, isn't it? Look at that. It's the only well-maintained fence in Queensland.'

He stopped at a hole to tie his pink inspector's tape onto the wire so the patrolman, travelling an hour behind us, could repair the break. 'It starts off as a goanna hole, then it's a kangaroo hole and before you know it you've got dogs going through it.'

There is no doubt Stanley is a perfectionist and his wife says he is the most cunning man she has ever known. I could see that his mind was like a dog trap. He had so far remembered every detail about my family, where I lived, the people I had met along the fence. Sometimes he would become very quiet as if chewing something over and then ask a detailed question to clarify a point. Most of all, he appears acutely aware of anything that seems untrue. He is a walking lie detector.

In twenty years Stanley has driven 1.4 million kilometres and has only had one accident. I told him how annoyed I was at myself for not having a second spare tyre and he surprised me by saying that he never carries a second wheel. His men drive around the fence in modified four-wheel-drives, loaded with safety and survival equipment. Stanley's car has all the mod-cons you would expect to see in a city car. Sitting beside that charismatic bulldozer of a man, listening to his besotted description of the beauty of the fence, I felt truly safe. Many of his men told me of experiencing a similar sensation even while Stanley pushed the car's speedo until it was at snapping point.

He was, I thought to myself, a mixture of Ned Kelly and Robert Duvall's air cavalry colonel in *Apocalypse Now*. He left school at fifteen to run cattle stations in the Kimberley for eleven years. When he returned, his brother, a patrolman, helped him get a job on the fence. Both his mother and father were also boundary riders. After a difficult year spent as his father's offsider, Stanley moved to Quilpie where he ran the western fence for four years. His wife, too, began work on the Barrier Fence. It was during that period in Quilpie, while still in his twenties, that his skills came to the attention of one of Australia's most eccentric and successful politicians, the peanut-farming premier, Joh Bjelke-Petersen. Sir Joh told his bureaucrats to make the infamously tough, youthful Stanley the boss of the fence. He was, the premier is reported to have said, the man who will fix it.

We passed paddocks littered with dirty salt licks, dumped by the farmers to ensure that their stock get to replenish vital minerals. After two hours, a sweeping escarpment reared up in front of us. The fence went over it but the maintenance track veered off to one side. 'It's a twelve-kilometre detour to get over that,' Stanley said glumly. 'There used to be a track that I made up there but it's impassable now.' He pointed to a scar that looked like a rockslide. 'It hasn't been driven for four years.' At the bottom of the cliff the old track was blocked off by a fallen tree. Stanley clambered out and began tugging at the trunk. I squinted up at the route he had carved into the escarpment. It looked like a field of boulders and I knew Stanley wasn't lying when he said he had nearly killed himself bulldozing the shortcut. 'OK,' he said, 'let's give it a go.'

Stanley put the car into four-wheel-drive, backed up then floored it towards the Jabinda jump-up. The car was slipping around, spitting out rocks and he was hanging onto the wheel as if wrestling a steer. At the halfway point the car was at an angle that made me feel I was rock climbing not driving, but we were not moving. There was no hope of reversing—if we lost momentum the car would tip backwards. Stanley pushed the accelerator deep into the carpet and somehow the wheels found something to grip on, launching us over the last ledge and onto the summit. He whooped with joy. 'Did you think we would make it?' he asked. I answered truthfully that I believed we would. Not because what we had done was necessarily possible but because I was in a car with a man who had travelled over a million Dog Fence kilometres and who had been excused from normal physical limitations.

At the top Stanley rolled a cigarette, cut great chunks of lamb for a crusty sandwich and sat on a tree looking across the Barcoo floodplain. 'I have been going up and down the line for twenty years. When I first came here the scrub was growing through the netting, thick like the hair on a dog's back. The first thing I had to do was bulldoze a track along 5000 kilometres of fence—two and a half thousand one way, two and a half thousand back. How many times have I sat here in this spot on this log? Fucking hundreds. In this job you are out here all the time. You are out here all the time on your own.'

Nothing, I remembered, is an exaggeration. If Stanley said he had sat and looked at that view hundreds of times then that is exactly what had happened. If he said the fence was once overgrown with scrub then it was. If anyone on Earth had the capacity to blaze a track and back across half a continent then it was Stanley.

An hour later we were in the main drag of Tambo. Emus were crossing the road opposite the post office. After refuelling we headed to the pub. Stanley knew the barman and the pair shared a laugh. Stanley's chortle filled up the whole room. We headed back to the fence where we found a flock of emus bigger by far than the mob I had seen the day before. They were running through the scrub on a hill beside the fence. They took contours as if their bodies were moulded into the scree—no matter how rough the ground, somehow their heads remained totally poised and level. The big mob had now formed into a dusty sea of birds about 200 metres long and ten metres wide. 'How many do you reckon there are?' Stanley said, looking as awed as I was.

'Hundreds, maybe five hundred.'

The emus were so tightly packed that when I tried to count the birds just in front of the bullbar there were dozens. It was more likely that there were thousands of birds. We were behind them and Stanley was determined to pass. Some were beginning to lose their rhythmic poise and their legs were wobbling like puppets. Others simply shook their vast grass-skirt behinds and sat down to die. Weaving through them, moving at around 30 kilometres per hour, Stanley did his best to make sure none got hit but it was like trying to run

Emus trying to find a way to escape the drought.

through a rainstorm without getting wet. They would suddenly break from the pack and slam into the bullbar before being sucked underneath the chassis and spat out at the back of the car with various degrees of injury. 'This is a natural disaster, Jim. This is a disaster. Waddya reckon, Jim, it's a disaster, isn't it?'

On the radio word came that a patrolman further east had been forced to open a gate in an attempt to funnel the birds away from the Barrier Fence. He estimated that up to a thousand emus were banked up, waiting to get out.

The mobs kept joining together as they had a few days earlier west of the Landsborough Highway. Soon this group was a kilometre long and comprised 3000 to 4000 emus.

We drove through a gate, changing sides to the outside of the fence. Now we had the Dog Fence between us and the birds and the track on our side was empty of life. As soon as the car was no longer behind them the emus stopped running. 'I've never seen emus this thick,' Stanley mused. 'Look what they're doing to the fence.' The cattleman in Stanley burst through. 'I'm going to get these emus away from the fence,' he declared. He pressed his hand to the horn and held it there, producing a deafening noise that made the emus bolt again. 'How do you like herding emus with Jerry?' Stanley called out to me over the din. I could see that he was torn between the fun of chasing thousands of emus along the Dog Fence and the knowledge that if the birds were to stay in that spot for even a few more days the fence would fall down.

The head of the mob came to a private boundary fence that ran perpendicular to the Dog Fence, and where the structures met the birds piled up as if stuck in a mosh pit. Some died and some scrambled over the dead birds to escape Stanley's horn. Most, however, forced themselves through the boundary fence's wire, thrashing and kicking until the wire released them. One bird miraculously jumped onto the back of two others like an Aussie Rules player and then leapt onto a pole on the Dog Fence where it stood delicately balanced. As we drove past it, horn blaring, the emu flipped backwards, landed on its feet and bounded off into the scrub.

By this time the mob was kilometres long, with several hundred out front still holding their stride. The landscape near Tambo is undulating and as far as I could see, up and down the two rises in front of us, was a wall of birds. Hundreds of emus were now collapsing onto the ground from exhaustion where they would almost certainly die. Another perpendicular boundary fence appeared ahead of us. This was more solid and, in the first act of self-preservation I had seen by emus that day, the mob veered away. Stanley sat there with his hand still on the horn. Thousands of emus were sprinting away under a low, dirty cloud of desert soil. We discovered that we had been chasing the birds for over ten kilometres and for at least half an hour. Of all the sights I had seen none so clearly demonstrated the immensity of the drought.

On our way to camp Stanley told me about the worst crisis he had ever had to manage on the fence, in the days when the Queenslanders had caravans instead of dongas. Two patrolmen—an older and a younger man—were working on the fence. The wife of the older patrolman was staying at the camp with them. The older man left to do a tour of inspection on his own and when he came back unexpectedly he found his wife in bed with his partner. The husband pulled a gun and shoved it into the mouth of the younger man. A third patrolman came by and walked in on the drama. Jerry was contacted and sped to the scene. Once he arrived, the gun was put away and the two patrolmen were separated. The younger man was sent to a run along the other end of the fence. Nobody called the police. The husband and wife stayed together.

CHAPTER 13

PICCANINNY DAWN

I have never met anyone who has built something as big as Jerry Stanley. He not only expects his fence to be perfect, he also expects his dongas to be the best workman's huts in Australia, and that is what they are.

That first night with Jerry we stayed in a hut near the Yandarlo homestead. Over the last 600 kilometres of the Barrier Fence, Stanley has negotiated the right to accommodate his men virtually on the doorstep of the farmers whose properties the fence passes through, ensuring access to electricity. Each one of the dongas has been begged, borrowed or stolen and has a history behind it that makes Jerry swoon with happiness. Outside one particularly well-maintained hut called Barn Go he asked me to photograph him so he could show his wife. I told him that if they ever shut the fence down, the Queensland government will own a top-shelf chain of huts for tourists.

Stanley checks the dongas for cleanliness and once a year

his wife Marie does a run where she meticulously notes any mess or damage. Stanley expects to see homely touches—fresh paint, homemade bush furniture, ingenious barbecues, water put out for wallabies and birds and a clean stove. 'Look at that,' he said beckoning me into the hut's kitchen. 'There's not a mark around that burner. That makes me very happy.'

The hot water system at Yandarlo was a wood-fired donkey and we cooked dinner on coals and talked for hours. I was starting to really like him. I had been told that Stanley would do anything for you as long as you never let him down. For the first time since my days with Sandow I felt as though I could relax, let my guard down and be myself.

Stanley told me that he had recently been interviewed for a documentary. After it was screened the television station and police received numerous calls that he fitted the description of the Peter Falconio murderer. The police interviewed him and requested DNA samples which he refused to provide. He had no alibi for the day in question. While chewing on a chilli olive he said that he would give DNA in the next week or so to get the police off his back.

Stanley could see I was a different kind of man from him but he didn't care that I had ten thumbs and approached the opening of every gate as if it were a Rubik's cube. Again and again he laughed long and hard at my puzzlement over various things to do with the fence but I never felt he was laughing out of contempt.

Once in a *New Yorker* magazine I saw a cartoon of a cat talking to a dog. The cat explained to the dog that the difference between them was that while the dog would eat the cat's food, the cat would never, *ever* eat the dog's food. In some ways that was how it was with Jerry and me. I enjoyed the hearty barbecues, the beer, the coffee, the roast lamb and tomato sandwiches. Whatever I pulled out of my food box, however, was a different matter. He refused to eat my yoghurt or my tuna and described my apricot juice as 'Cooper's Creek water'. He ate my olives but they played havoc with his 'guts' all night. One thing we shared and talked about at length was the difficult relationship we have had with our fathers. In 1951 in Roma, Stanley's father was charged with stealing cattle but the court found him not guilty. Stanley and his father never got on and even on his deathbed Noel Stanley refused to make peace with his son. Yet there was one thing that both men respected about each other—each had a reputation for extraordinary toughness. On several occasions Stanley said of his father, 'He was hard, hard, hard.'

That night Stanley shared a story which helped illustrate why he is so concerned about safety issues and why he is such a fierce family man. In the Kimberley, after a long muster away from his young wife and son, he returned home to find their eleven-month-old baby had been electrocuted. They later discovered this was due to the homestead's faulty wiring.

Long before dawn Stanley was awake and preparing to leave. 'I haven't been up after 6 am for ten years. At home I shower every morning religiously at 5.' We drank a coffee, swept and washed the donga, then headed off. As a city dweller, with three children to get ready for school, I rarely have time, or the will, to see the sunrise. The full subtlety of the morning is invisible in a city anyway. With these Queensland patrolmen, however, I was becoming used to rising a couple of hours before the sun, yet I had no word for the morning's equivalent of twilight. I asked Stanley if he knew what it was called. 'Piccaninny dawn', he said. I later read Lucy Walker's description of the light before sunrise in her 1975 book, *Runaway Girl*: 'The piccaninny dawn was growing up fast. First in its strange other-world way it had become temporarily darker, then quite suddenly the sky, and all the world became grey. Next pale grey. Then there was light. It was daybreak.'

Back on the fence we passed hundreds of emus, but there weren't as many as the previous day. We travelled through an uncleared block that Stanley said had one of the greatest concentrations of dingoes—inside and outside the fence—in Queensland. The grazier on whose land we were now driving refused to use poison baits. Even worse, according to Stanley, new anti-landclearing laws would protect the virgin brigalow scrub and it would remain a haven for wild dogs.

Beside a long straight section of the fence, surrounded on both sides by low forest, Stanley threw on the brakes. A pack of dogs was working a mob of emus against the fence. They were inside the barrier. I could see two dogs. Stanley saw three and was certain that at least one other was involved in the hunt. The birds wheeled in dizzy circles while the dogs, with fangs bared, snapped at their heels. Stanley put his foot to the floor and sped forward. One of the dogs fled into the scrub at once. It resembled a dingo but was an alsatian cross. The second dog, which was a dingo, froze on the edge of the track. Stanley aimed his car at the animal and was now at full throttle, the fence passing in a blur. Ten metres away Stanley fishtailed the four-wheel-drive, hoping to sideswipe the dog and avoid the tree it was sitting beside. At the last second, with petulant casualness and a last look straight into our eyes, the dingo jogged off. 'That pisses me off!' Stanley exclaimed. 'At least three dogs and what makes it worse is that they were inside the fence. If I'd had my gun I'd have been able to shoot two of them easily.'

An emu was sitting on its haunches, injured and immobilised, but not fatally. We drove on. It was almost certain that as soon as we disappeared the dogs would be back and the bird would be killed.

We travelled into a different landscape of forty-metre-tall eucalypts and grass trees with the girth of power poles. The soil too had changed from dust to white sand. Some of the toughest fence that Stanley had to bring to heel in the 1980s was in this area. The only way to keep weeds and regrowth from overpowering the structure is by annual poisoning and regular bulldozing. Nothing is allowed to grow within metres of the fence, with one exception. When Stanley first started on the fence a young kurrajong sapling was growing beside the wire and today it is twenty metres tall. 'When I started the tree was lower than the fence. It's a beautiful tree and no machine's allowed to go near it. Nobody's allowed to touch it.' Near the kurrajong the fence-posts still had the remnants of the original telephone party-line attached.

At lunchtime we stopped under two giant bottle trees. 'Look up,' Jerry said. In the crown of the tree was an old spring bed base. Stanley explained how the old doggers used to tie their bitches to the base of the trunk when they were in heat. The dogger would then climb up on a mattress and wait in relative comfort for the dingoes to come in on the scent of the female. When they got close enough they were shot.

The following morning on Morley Station, north of Mitchell, we came across a scene of emu carnage, again inside the fence, in another forested area infamous for dogs. Stanley climbed out of the car and tried to reconstruct events as if it were a crime scene. He stuck his hand under the dead emu's feathers where there was a massive chest wound. 'It's still warm. This must have just happened. Fucking dogs.' There were dingo tracks everywhere in the sandy soil. 'The emu's come running out of the scrub and run into the fence and the

A dogger's cubby. A bed base located in a tree was used as a platform for dingo hunting.

dogs have got it on the rebound.' The kill was spread out over ten to fifteen metres—Stanley found a plug of blood, flesh and feathers in the sand nearby. He kicked it, upset by what he had seen.

On the radio news a few minutes later we heard that Steve Fossett, who had planned to complete his round-the-world balloon trip in South Australia, was expected to land somewhere west of Quilpie that morning. Stanley told his men to keep an eye out for it. 'What balloon?' Fleggy asked. 'I've been out on the fence and I haven't heard the news for a few days.' At about 8 am word came that it had landed at Durham Downs and the cattle station was transformed into a media circus.

Days after this a gust of wind carried the empty balloon east into the desert. Soon afterwards Fleggy and Gray were grading forty kilometres north of the Wilson Overflow. Gray spotted it first—a strange object a few hundred metres inside the Barrier Fence. 'That's no fucking weather balloon,' Fleggy exclaimed, 'that's Steve Fossett's balloon that blew away.'

The two men struggled to load it into the back of the ute and kept it in Quilpie for a week before contacting a radio show to announce their discovery. Reluctantly they handed the valuable souvenir over to the woman from whom it had escaped.

Soon after lunch on Thursday, 4 July 2002, we arrived at Roma. Stanley booked me into a pub in the centre of town and I went in search of my four-wheel-drive, which had been driven from Blackall by the car hire company. I would be able to use it for the last 600 kilometres of the Dog Fence.

In Roma I had meetings with the two men who have the daunting job of formally holding Stanley's leash—senior bureaucrat in the Queensland Department of Natural Resources, Jim Herbert, and chairman of the Maranoa Graziers Association, Don Compagnoni.

Compagnoni and Stanley have developed a deep respect and trust for each other. Compagnoni told me a story about how a grazier was annoyed at the muddy mess Stanley and a convoy, including Compagnoni, were making at a creek crossing after rain some years ago. Stanley was on one side of the Dog Fence and the cocky was on the other. A brawl broke out between the two but no punches could be landed because of the wire between them. 'The fence did its job that day,' Compagnoni said.

'There's the passionate side to Jerry. He desperately wants to do the job. He hasn't been transformed by the bureaucratic system. There are lots of things you have got to do out there on the fence that are not illegal, but you know how it is. Jerry seems to get by.'

Jim Herbert is a small man and, like me, has soft points in all the places where Jerry's body is as hard as steel. There was a desk between us and it was hard to believe that in a few hours I had moved from a world where dingoes chased and mauled emus to Herbert's paper-cluttered office. 'Jerry loves the job,' Herbert told me, 'because he still gets to do the things he loves doing. He's the boss but he can still get out there and spend all day working on the bulldozer. What I like about the fence is that you drive along it and kilometre after kilometre is the kind of fence that you dream of having.'

The next morning I met up with patrolmen Max Lewis and Stephen Edgley. It was still dark when I arrived at their camp but they were busy cleaning up. This was the last day of their run which would take them through to the very small town of Injune. They would cover over seventy kilometres of rough country, but in places the Dog Fence now passed within metres of farmhouse kitchen windows, travelled over driveways and passed under powerlines.

The number of gates was increasing exponentially. Back in the Great Victoria Desert with Bill Sandow I opened one gate in 1000 kilometres. From Roma on I had been warned that there were often two or three gates every kilometre. Now I was seeing mothers packing their children off to school, farmers dashing off on business. People waved at me as I passed, assuming that I was part of the official Dog Fence traffic. I spent the day watching Edgley and Lewis skilfully repair the fence using beautiful iron tools. Jerry's men have a tool for almost every problem that the fence throws up, such as a portable pile driver for fixing star pickets into rock-hard soil.

It was my last night in Roma. I had 5100 kilometres of the fence behind me. In Queensland I had passed through many different ecosystems, across landscapes that seemed to morph every few kilometres. I met patrolman Joshua Davie in the queue of a fast-food shop. I had last spoken to him the morning I left Camp 16. Standing in the line he confirmed my worst fears. All the patrolmen had been following my progress via the radio as if it were a soap opera. 'This is the guy I was telling you about,' Davie told his wife. 'The one that had the problem with his wheel.'

I stopped at Jerry's home for a quick beer and to map out the final few days. I was stunned to discover that Jerry has a pet chihuahua called Nigel. His wife, Marie, surprised me further when she confessed in a soft voice that Jerry lets it sleep in his bed. Man's relationship with dogs must be one of the most complicated in the animal kingdom.

Marie is beautiful, with brown hair and an intelligent and kind face. She was quiet and, although very petite, she is clearly a woman every bit as strong as her husband. She runs the home and the Dog Fence office—everything about both was neat and perfect.

I had to travel over 200 kilometres through dozens of private properties to get from Injune to Miles. Even though civilisation was closing in fast, the Dog Fence was now crossing the Great Dividing Range and each kilometre east the track got rougher. Stanley had given me detailed instructions about the complicated route that the fence would take that first morning out of Roma. His voice came over the radio at 7.30 asking me how I was going. I was lost and for the next half-hour he and the patrolman whose route I was on guided me through a maze of fences, gates, private farmyards, over creeks, over pipes, past roadworks, countless grids and piles of old cars. In places the fence ran beside sealed road for kilo-metres. I pulled into the Dulacca Hotel after dark where, apart from exceptional hospitality, the most memorable feature was a padded, plastic toilet seat that slowly exhaled perfumed, soapy bubbles from a tiny hole when I sat on it.

Stanley was relieved when I rang to say I had made it to Dulacca unscathed. We arranged to meet the next morning in a park outside Miles. I would leave my car there and once again I would be in the safe hands of Jerry Stanley.

Next morning I offloaded my gear into Stanley's car and within half an hour we were back on the Barrier Fence, crossing a precipitous watercourse named Dogwood Creek by Ludwig Leichhardt when he explored the area in 1844. It was mostly dry when we went through, but on one occasion Stanley and his men took a four-wheel-drive along the fence and for three kilometres were sitting with the water 'up to our guts inside the cabin'.

We had two days to make it to Jandowae where the fence ended and my journey would be completed. Having reached Dulacca I had a paltry 200 kilometres to go. That morning we talked about how Jerry had won an Australia Day honours award for his services to the Dog Fence and how the graziers with whom he has such a love-hate relationship, had presented him with a beautiful landscape painting to thank him for rebuilding the fence. I also discovered that the state government has approached him to help with the construction of a special predator-proof fence around the last population of the critically endangered northern hairy-nosed wombats. The construction of that fence is one of the most vital and desperately needed conservation tasks in Australia.

On Colamba Station, just north of Miles, we came across an immaculately maintained metre-high fence branching off from the Barrier Fence. 'That's the Rabbit Proof Fence,' Stanley declared. That fence is 500 kilometres long and runs down to Hungerford on the New South Wales–Queensland border but is not to be confused with its more famous Western Australian counterpart. It has its own team of people who maintain it. Looking at the Rabbit Proof Fence winding off into the distance I realised that the Dog Fence resembles a major river with many tributaries: suburban paling fences join onto millions of kilometres of privately owned wire fences on farms, which in turn connect onto the government-run fences like the Dog Fence and the Rabbit Fence. As the Dog Fence heads westward into the deserts the tributaries decrease and for the last thousand kilometres before hitting the Great Australian Bight it is the only line across the sand.

Stanley showed me an innovation he has designed to stop dingoes crossing cattle grids. 'This guy was getting his arse chewed off by dingoes,' Stanley said, waving his arm at a property inside the fence, 'but since I put this in he hasn't lost anything.'

He pointed to a small cage with a solar panel situated beside the cattle grid. Inside the cage was a box which emitted a high frequency whistle. The machines are specially built and cost about $500 each. They have been so successful in deterring dingoes that Stanley has ordered sufficient numbers to place one at every cattle grid on the Barrier Fence. He is also recommending that the South Australian government consider using the high frequency whistle. He knows it works, he told me, because he tested the device on Nigel. When the dog heard the noise it bolted in pain.

What Stanley seemed especially proud of, however, was that the device was so neat and clean. 'See, there's no rust on the box protecting the power. I got the patrolman to paint the cage and he dusts it every time he comes past. It looks like somebody looks after it.'

Just before reaching my last camp on the Dog Fence Stanley stopped at what looked like a mailbox stuck on the fence. The little box was once used for the cockies and patrolmen to communicate with each other. Brief messages would be left about maintenance work that needed doing or equipment that was required, but the system broke down because often the notes were abusive. Stanley said he had something to show me. He opened the lid of the old mailbox and produced a rough-edged fragment of a Benson & Hedges cigarette carton. On it was inscribed a joyous note written by Jerry's mum, Joyce. 'Noel, Jerry, Joyce, Leanne, Marie. We were here as fencers in 1983.' I felt transported back to a moment when the Stanley family tried to immortalise their time on the fence. I wrote my own note and dropped it into the box.

'I remember that day with the box of smokes,' Stanley said. 'We would work with Dad for a week and he wouldn't speak. He would go a week without saying anything but hello.'

A few kilometres later we passed a pair of old jeans strung up on the fence. 'They fell apart one day in 1988 and I tossed them onto the fence. They're still there. All the boys know to leave them alone. I like all those little treats that we've got around—they're all landmarks.'

A bushfire was burning to the west, and that night at Yapunya, forty kilometres north of Chinchilla, the sun set behind the fence like an eye on fire. I felt both sad and excited. Stanley was still refusing to tell me what the end of the fence looked like. Getting to the end had taken on a weird significance and if I had to crawl on my hands and knees to reach it then that is what I would do.

Stanley got in his swag soon after dinner and we started talking. 'The Barrier Fence is a great departmental asset,' he told me as he lay there smoking, looking exhausted. 'If they ever don't want it then I hope they just tell me because a fence is something you have got to maintain. It's like a yard fence, if you don't look after it then it will fall down. If you can't find the money then you're better off just walking away. You give me the money and I'll manage it. I've spent twenty years constructing this asset for the department.' There was a tinge of sadness in his words and I sensed he felt his work was not as appreciated as it used to be. Once, the only law Stanley had to obey was keeping a wall of wire and posts dog-proof. If that was done then nobody asked any questions. Nowadays his life was increasingly consumed by reports, policies and administration.

I moved my mat out on to the verandah, but stared at the stars for ages before I could fall asleep. Only one more day to go on the fence and I realised I had seen no Aborigines other than those in the car which roared through the scrub on my first day with Sandow. Not one indigenous Australian is employed on the Queensland fence and, while I must have passed countless places of cultural importance to Aborigines, the fence patrolmen and inspectors in each of the three states could tell me next to nothing of this. It was disappointing though not surprising when one considers that the Dog Fence protects an industry which has done more than any other to dispossess Aboriginal people.

In the morning Stanley was dumbstruck to discover that his car battery was flat. It was my fault; he had asked me to turn the car fridge off but I had turned the knob the wrong way. In the freezing pre-dawn mist Stanley was suffering a sensation rare to him—helplessness. We waited until we could see a sign of life in the farmhouse nearby then Stanley walked over and asked for their jumper leads. It was the kind of thing that he hates doing. Stanley knows that the farmers who let his men stay on their land are doing him an enormous favour and he does not like to push the friendship. He demands that his staff be on their best behaviour when they camp at the huts and he discourages patrolmen from making any demands on their hosts. Within a few minutes his turbocharged four-wheel-drive had roared back into life and we were ready. 'This is your last leg of the Dog Fence,' he said to me as we pulled out.

We skirted through thick, rocky forests and on top of one cleared hill we passed house-sized stands of prickly pear. We met a man tending his cattle right beside the fence. He had two kelpies and was using them to control his stock while he fed the cattle by hand. This was the Dog Fence equivalent of a Hollywood tour where visitors drive through the suburbs and are shown the homes of movie stars. 'This guy was a minister in the Bjelke-Petersen government,' Stanley would say. 'This was his brother's place.' At another point the Dog Fence wrapped around some cattle yards. 'I don't like to encourage that,' Stanley mumbled. In one spot the fence marked somebody's front yard and had a letterbox poking through. The densely rainforested Bunya Mountains were now visible and in some places planted bunya pines were growing.

We finally entered a property called Dunleavin, which was infested with prickly pear. We left its boundaries and travelled on the outside of the fence down a rustic, sealed road called Fletcher's Lane. It ran for about two kilometres.

'Mate, I wasn't expecting to feel anything except excited at this moment,' I said to Jerry, 'but I feel sad.'

'Have you noticed how in the last half-hour we've stopped talking?' Jerry replied. 'I've just been watching you and you have been getting quieter and quieter.'

'This is the end of an adventure for me,' I said. 'I don't get to live like this in Sydney. Being on the fence is so simple.'

The landscape was opening up fast and I could sense that my journey would be over at any moment.

'We've only a couple of minutes to go. When we get to the top of this hill you'll be able to see it.' He paused. 'There it is.'

'That's it?' I asked.

Ahead of me was a twenty-metre-tall casuarina. The fence came to an abrupt end in the middle of nowhere, by the tree.

I asked Jerry if I could cut a piece off the end of it and he asked me to sever him a section too. I told him how bemused Sandow was when I asked to cut the piece from the other end 5400 kilometres away. 'I don't think it's strange,' he said, putting his souvenir in his jacket. 'I understand completely.' This place was warm, cloudless and a world away from the Great Australian Bight. Not a single vehicle went past, no people were in sight.

'Before we finish up I want to show you the place where

The last post—and nothing is there to prevent dogs walking around the end of it.

the fence *should* end,' Stanley said, calling me back to the car.

Stanley wants to extend the finishing point another four or five kilometres along Fletcher's Lane before he retires. He wants closure, completion and achievement. He also wants a sign and is negotiating the construction of a billboard so that tourists can come and see the end of the Dog Fence.

'If I can get the patrolmen to get twenty metres or so done each week, then we will get to where it should end within a couple of years.'

He showed me an existing but dilapidated netting fence

which he and his men reckon can be restored for less than $4000 per kilometre. If the plan goes ahead the new termination point would occur beside an enormous box tree. Across the road—literally—begin the Darling Downs. The downs are among the richest agricultural lands in Australia—and free of dogs. There's also a cattle grid there which theoretically means that no dogs could get past.

'If a dog ever got out there, he'd be lost,' Jerry said pointing towards a laser-levelled paddock so vast that its horizon was a shimmering mirage. 'He'd get run over by a header or a combine or something. There's not a tree between here and Toowoomba.'

He sighed. 'I am happy—not just with the fence but also with the grading, the track work and the accommodation. But I've got to get the fence to here so I have achieved something.'

We drove back to the current end of the fence. Before I stepped out of the car I was surprised to see Stanley's great, hard hand held up in front of me. 'There you are, Jim. Just think, the next gate you open will be the one into your yard at home. You made it. Congratulations.'

EPILOGUE

Six months later, on 4 December 2002 at 7.40 pm there was to be a total solar eclipse. The path of totality—the narrow band within which the sun would be completely obscured by the moon—would cross the Dog Fence three times. Nothing short of a planetary cataclysm would prevent the cosmic coincidence from occurring. Scientists had calculated to the second exactly when and where the eclipse would be visible. It would first darken the Dog Fence at the southern extreme of the Great Victoria Desert thirty kilometres north-east of Ceduna. A few seconds later the immense shadow of the moon, travelling at 20,000 kilometres per hour, would hit the wire a second time north of the Flinders Ranges near Mount Hopeless. Finally the path of totality would end at Cameron Corner—the junction of the borders of South Australia, New South Wales and Queensland.

When I first saw a map of the shadow's route early in 2002 I was about to leave Ceduna with Bill Sandow. I was struck by how close the path of the eclipse matched the route of the Dog Fence—except with all the kinks and corners taken out by some divine bureaucratic force. I felt compelled to embark on my first eclipse chase.

I planned to travel to Ceduna on 3 December. I called Bill to let him know I was on my way in case he felt like a cold beer and a catch-up chat. As soon as he answered the phone I felt awash with good memories of travelling together. He was, however, planning a spell of long-deserved leave and predicted that cloud would spoil the show.

I spoke to Ricky Hammat, the man who had first introduced me to the South Australian fence, about accommodation. Tens of thousands of people were expected to converge on Ceduna so I chose a remote little hill, out of town and a few kilometres away from the fence, on which to spend the evening of 4 December.

When I flew into Adelaide the news was not good. The Bureau of Meteorology was forecasting heavy cloud cover at Ceduna. I was travelling with one of my oldest friends, Bentley Dean. In the carpark at Adelaide airport, we pulled out the map I used back in February and decided on a change of plan. We would drive north into the desert towards Mount Hopeless. The name immediately captured Ben's imagination. And my attempts to climb it earlier in the year had been thwarted by a shortage of time and fuel. I called Doug Sprigg, the owner of Arkaroola in the Flinders Ranges, to confirm that the eclipse was crossing just to his north.

We pulled into Arkaroola well after dark, but eclipse mania was heavy in the air and Sprigg was busy in his observatory with astronomers from all over the world. Early the next morning we went down to his quarters and into his office, where he printed us off a topographic map of the exact path of totality. It was fifty kilometres wide and it crossed the Dog Fence on the boundary between Michael Sheehan's property at Moolawatana and Mount Hopeless.

We drove beside Lake Frome for several hours and reached Sheehan's property late in the morning to seek permission to drive across his land. I told him how intimidated I was during my first meeting because of his reputation for loathing both tourists and dingoes. He smiled and replied, 'If I had a nuclear bomb in those days I would have nuked them, but now they don't worry me. I don't mind seeing the odd dingo.'

About ten kilometres north of his homestead we crossed the Dog Fence, turned off the road onto the maintenance track and headed into the predicted path of totality. I had last driven through this area at 2 am when it had started to rain the February night I had camped on Yerilla Creek.

The further north-east the eclipse path travelled the narrower it became and the shorter the period of totality. There was not a cloud in the sky, however, and by lunchtime we had chosen our spot. We drank two bottles of red wine and ate bread rolls stuffed with salted meat and sundried tomatoes. The landscape all around us was treeless, gibber desert, scattered with crystals. The wind was hot and hard, whistling through the Dog Fence, which at that point is electrified and modern. We must have been two of the most isolated eclipse watchers for the third total solar eclipse of the twenty-first century.

At 6.40 pm the moon started to move across the sun. Through our ridiculous-looking eclipse glasses we watched our star become an ever-diminishing crescent. The strangest dusk I had ever seen began to take hold. It became dark without our shadows lengthening. They instead changed colour and blurred, looking so different from normal that I would not have been surprised if they had gotten up and walked away. In the last few minutes before totality the upside-down crescent of the sun became a blinding half ring.

Just after 7.40 pm a rushing shadow sped across the desert and the last speck of the unblocked sun disappeared with a blink. Instantaneously, and as if by some immense act of magic, our star was utterly transformed from an object we take for granted into the most glorious sight. Great ribs of ghostly, glowing light stretched across the sky for hundreds of kilometres. In that moment I am certain that I saw the famed Bailey's Beads—a burst of light as the sun's rays travel through the gaps between the mountains on the moon. The ultra-hot corona glowed with a beauty so intense that not only could I see it, I felt as though I could hear it crackling.

Most amazingly, I was staring directly at the sun. It looked cool and close, like an eye surrounded by eyelashes lit by colours that I had never known existed.

After ten seconds of totality, the sun burst through from the underside of the black disc of the moon, which instantly vanished as intense solar radiation returned. Soon after 8 pm the sun—now a partially eclipsed right-way up crescent—set with a final dramatic twinkle behind the Dog Fence.

An eclipse reinforces the fact that we live in a universe, and that we do not control it. At the same time we cannot even begin to conceive what is at the end of the cosmos. Could it be a wall—the greatest fence ever created?

ACKNOWLEDGMENTS

Thanks to my wife Prue for understanding and supporting my crazy dream of driving the Dog Fence. She listened to my stories, read the manuscript, watched our bank balance plummet yet never once did she discourage me. My children, Angus, Finn and Sophie, had to tolerate a lot of childcare juggling while I was away. In this regard special thanks go to Ngaire Hasse and Brenda Hungerford. I also thank Ngaire for all the support she has given to me and my family during the writing process.

Readers would have had to struggle through considerably more waffle without the help of editor Melanie Ostell. I thank her and the rest of the team at Text Publishing.

Close friends Stuart Cohen and Toby Whitelaw encouraged me and spent endless hours talking me through the project. Bentley Dean was crazy enough to come on an eclipse chase into the desert and saved the day with his easy manner and laidback approach to cosmic phenomena.

The hospitality shown to me on the fence was humbling. I was given a roof over my head by the Rankin family, Peter Paisley, the Croziers, Peter Flegg, Phil Dickie and Susan Brown and Ingrid Witte. Many others offered accommodation which I had to refuse because of time constraints. I am grateful to everyone for the showers, the meals, the sandwiches and coffee given to me *wherever* I went.

This book would not have been possible without fence inspectors Bill Sandow, Peter Flegg and Jerry Stanley. I thank them all for their patience, advice and assistance. Thanks, too, to Len Dixon who first introduced me to the Dog Fence a decade ago and who so readily gave me permission to travel through his patrol this time around.

Marie Stanley helped me with maps and Nick Lomb at Sydney Observatory assisted with the science of eclipses. I am indebted to the research of Phil Gee for much of the historical material in South Australia, especially for the country between Roxby Downs and Arkaroola. I also relied on the work of Roland Breckwoldt, John Read, Daniel Lunney and the team at the University of New England. The staff at the Charles Rasp Library in Broken Hill were helpful in sourcing the material concerning the Martin girls. Ben Kear, Doug Sprigg, Ricky Hammat, the Mohrs, the Dobbins family, Alasdair McGregor, Tim Flannery and many others also provided assistance.

A debt must also be acknowledged to Dinah Percival, co-author of *Fence People*, whose 1989 book provided many insights.

BIBLIOGRAPHY

PAPERS, JOURNALS, NEWSPAPERS AND MAGAZINES

Adnyamathanha Art and Dreaming: Aboriginal Heritage of the Flinders and Gammon Ranges, South Australian National Parks and Wildlife Service, 1989.

Annual Report of the Dog Fence Board 2000–2001, South Australian Government, 2001.

'Australia's Darkest and Brightest', *Atmosphere*, CSIRO newsletter, no. 12, April 2002.

Bates, Daisy, 'Hunting and Trapping the Dingo', *Western Mail*, 14 March 1914.

Bottroff, Clair, letter to his parents, Tarcoola, 1950.

Breckwoldt, Roland, 'Dingo!', *Geo Australasia*, vol. 8, no. 2, June/August 1986, pp. 16–33.

Cane, Scott, *Heritage Values of the Nullarbor Plain*, Department of the Arts, Sport, the Environment and Territories, 1992.

—— *Spinifex Stories, Myth Lines of the Great Victoria Desert and Nullarbor Plain*, Paupiyala Tjarutja and Australian Heritage Commission, 1996.

—— *Environmental, Anthropological and Archaeological Background to the Nullarbor Plains*, vols I and II, Anutech Pty Ltd, Canberra, 1988.

—— *An Anthropological Assessment of the Ooldea Ranges, South Australia*, report to Maralinga Tjarutja, 1990.

Duncan, Charles, 'Men on the Fence', *Geo Australasia*, vol. 16, no. 5, September/October 1994, pp. 88–101.

Early History of the Border Fences, pamphlet, Wild Dog Destruction Board, Broken Hill.

Gee, Philip, letter to Keith Greenfield, 18 December 1993.

Gee, Philip and Ifeta, 'John McDouall Stuart, South Australian Explorer: The Search for Wingilpin—Tracking Part of his 1858 Exploration', *South Australian Geographical Journal*, vol. 94, 1995, pp.18–35.

Guidelines for Surveyors in Re-establishing the Queensland–New South Wales Border, Queensland Dept of Natural Resources and NSW Dept of Information Technology and Management, 2000.

Hill, Kendall, 'No Stone Unturned Where Birdies Often Are

Galahs', *Sydney Morning Herald*, 29 April 2000, p. 1.

Kidman Centenary 1899–1999, Kidman Pastoral Company, Adelaide, 1999.

Lunney, Daniel, 'Causes of the Extinction of Native Mammals of the Western Division of New South Wales: An Ecological Interpretation of the Nineteenth Century Historical Record', *Rangelands*, no. 23, 2001, pp. 44–70.

Mars Society of Australia press release, 'Australian Mars Research Facility One Step Closer', 14 November 2001, or go to www.marssociety.org.

Martin, Colin, witness deposition concerning the deaths of Joyce and Suzanne Martin, 16 December 1959, South Australian Coroner's Office.

Neales, Sue, 'Kings in Grass Castles', *Outback*, no. 15, Feb/March 2001, pp. 32–60; no. 21, Feb/March 2002, pp. 32–69.

O'Neill, Thomas, 'Travelling the Australian Dog Fence', *National Geographic*, April 1997, pp. 18–37.

'Parents Near Death in Trek for Aid, Water', *Barrier Daily Truth*, Broken Hill, 17 December 1959.

Pickard, John, 'Trespass: Common Law, Government Regulations, and Fences in Colonial New South Wales, 1788–1828', *Journal of the Royal Australian Historical Society*, no. 84, 1998, pp. 131–39.

—— 'Fences: Ordinary Objects Integrating the History of Ordinary Landscapes', *Proceedings of the Annual Conference of the Royal Australian Historical Society*, Sydney, 1994.

—— 'Rural Fences: Perhaps the Most Common (and Most Commonly Neglected) Component of European Cultural Landscapes in Australia', *Historic Environment*, no. 13, 1997, pp. 19–22.

—— 'The First Fences: Fencing the Colony of New South Wales', *Agricultural History*, vol. 73, Winter, 1999.

Pople, A. R., Grigg, G. C., Cairns, S. C., Beard, L. A. and Alexander, P., 'Trends in the Numbers of Red Kangaroos and Emus on Either Side of the South Australian Dingo Fence: Evidence for Predator Regulation?', *Wildlife Research*, 2000, no. 27, pp. 269–76.

Queensland Dingo Barrier Fence, Natural Resources Queensland, Roma.

Read, John, 'Abundance and Recruitment Patterns of the Trilling Frog (*Neobatrachus centralis*) in the Australian Arid Zone', *Australian Journal of Zoology*, no. 47, 1999, pp. 393–404.

'Diet and Causes of Mortality of the Trilling Frog (*Neobatrachus centralis*)', *Herpetofauna*, no. 29 (1), 1999, pp. 13–18.

Review of the Dog Fence Act 1946, South Australian Government, July 2001.

'Salt Lake Helps Test Satellite Imager', *Atmosphere*, CSIRO newsletter, issue 11, October 2001.

'Sayings of the Week', *Sydney Morning Herald*, 4 November 1995, p. 32.

Short, Andrew, 'The Distribution and Impact of Carbonate Sands on Southern Australian Beach-Dune Systems', *Carbonate Beaches 2000*, international symposium, American Society of Civil Engineers and US Geological survey, Key Largo, 2000, pp. 1–42.

A Symposium on the Dingo, Chris Dickman and Daniel Lunney (eds), Royal Zoological Society of New South Wales, 2001.

Van Dyck, Steve, 'Budgerigars: Mini Aussie Megastars', *Australian Natural History*, Autumn, 1995, pp. 20–21.

'KFC with a Kick,' *Nature Australia*, Winter, 2000, pp. 20–21.

BOOKS

Astronomy 2002: A Practical Guide to the Night Sky, Glenn Dawes (ed.), Quasar Publishing, Sydney, 2001.

Bates, Daisy, *The Passing of the Aborigines*, Oxford University Press, Melbourne, 1944.

Beadell, Len, *Blast the Bush*, Rigby, Adelaide, 1967.

Breckwoldt, Roland, *A Very Elegant Animal the Dingo*, Angus & Robertson, Sydney, 1988.

Burrows, R. and Barton, A., *Henry Lawson: A Stranger in the Darling*, Angus & Robertson, Sydney, 1996.

Cane, Scott, *Pila Nguru: The Spinifex People*, Fremantle Arts Centre Press, Perth, 2002.

Corbett, Laurie, *The Dingo in Australia and Asia*, Cornell University Press, New York, 1995.

Explore the Flinders Ranges, Sue Barker (ed.), Royal Geographical Society of Australasia, Adelaide, 1995.

Flinders, Matthew, *Terra Australis: Matthew Flinders' Great Adventures in the Circumnavigation of Australia*, Tim Flannery (ed.), Text Publishing, Melbourne, 2000.

Giles, Ernest, *Australia Twice Traversed*, facsimile pub., vols I and II, Doubleday, Sydney, 1979.

Holden, Phillip, *Along the Dingo Fence*, Hodder & Stoughton, Sydney, 1991.

Latz, Peter, *Bushfires and Bushtucker: Aboriginal Plant Use in Central Australia*, IAD Press, Alice Springs, 1995.

Litchfield, Lois, *Marree and the Tracks beyond in Black and White*, self-published, Adelaide, 1983.

Lester, Yami, *Yami: The Autobiography of Yami Lester*, IAD Press, Alice Springs, 1993.

McDonald, Lorna, *West of Matilda: Outback Queensland 1890s–1990s*, Central Queensland University Press, Rockhampton, 2001.

Managing the Impacts of Dingoes and other Wild Dogs, Peter Fleming (ed.), Bureau of Rural Sciences, Canberra, 2001.

Menkhorst, Peter and Knight, Frank, *Mammals of Australia*, Oxford University Press, Melbourne, 2001.

Morton, Peter, *Fire across the Desert: Woomera and the Anglo-Australian Joint Project 1946–1980*, AGPS, Canberra, 1989.

Pearson, John, *Bluebird and the Dead Lake*, Text Publishing, Melbourne, 2002.

Percival, Dinah and Westney, Candida, *Fence People: Yarns from the Dingo Fence*, Hutchinson Australia, Sydney, 1989.

Pilkington, Doris and Nugi, Garimara, *Follow the Rabbit Proof Fence*, University of Queensland Press, Queensland, 1996.

Pizzey, Graham and Knight, Frank, *Field Guide to the Birds of Australia*, Angus & Robertson, Sydney, 1997.

Reardon, Mitch, *The Nullarbor*, Australian Geographic, Sydney, 1996.

Shephard, Mark, *The Great Victoria Desert*, Reed Books, Sydney, 1995.

—— *A Lifetime in the Bush: The Biography of Len Beadell*, Corkwood Press, Adelaide, 1998.

Short, Andy, *Beaches of the Southern Australian Coast and Kangaroo Island*, Australian Beach Safety and Management Project, Sydney, 2001.

Sprigg, Griselda and Maclean, Rod, *DUNE is a Four-Letter Word*, Wakefield Press, Adelaide, 2001.

Stuart, John McDouall, *Explorations in Australia*, Libraries Board of South Australia, Adelaide, 1975.

Walker, Lucy, *Runaway Girl*, Collins, London, 1975.

Walters, Berenice, *The Company of Dingoes: Two Decades with Our Native Dog*, Australian Native Dog Conservation Society Ltd, Bargo, 1995.

Yelland, Leith, *Holding the Line: A History of the South Australian Dog Fence Board, 1947–2000*, Primary Industries and Resources South Australia, Adelaide, 2001.

INDEX

References to photographs are in italics.

Aborigines 8–10, 19–20, 27, 30–32, 34, 42–43, 47–48, 53–55, 58–61, 66–67, 150, 240
Andrews, Francis 166
Anna Creek Station 88
Arid Recovery Reserve 119
Arkaroola Station 144, 247

Balharry, Michael 32
Barcoo River 216
Barwick, Darryl *190*
Bates, Daisy 30–31, 54
Beadell, Len 66
Beelitz, Keith 103, 108–13, *111*, 125
Billa Kalina Station 108, 114–15
Bjelke-Petersen, Joh 218
Black, Robert 190, *190*, 192
Blackall 213–14
Boland, Jeff 77
Boondoon 209, *210*
Borlace, Ross and Yvonne 32
Bottroff, Clair 94
Breckwoldt, Roland 10
brumbies 136, 154
budgerigars 32
Bulloo River 185–86
Burke and Wills 139
Burton, Len 65
bustards 21–22

camels 24–26, 37, 54, 68–70, *69*
Cameron, John 169
Cameron Corner 168–70
Campbell, Donald 129–31
Cane, Scott 7, 53, 55, 67
Carter, Jude 123
cats 63, 121
Ceduna 33–35
Chinaman's Hat Hill 112
Clayton Station 132
Colamba Station 237
Compagnoni, Don 233
Coober Pedy 80, 85–88
Cook, John 56
Corbett, Laurie 8
Crombie, Flo 101, 106–7
Crozier, Ben 159–60
Crozier, Randall 157–59
Crozier, Tanya 158

Davie, Joshua 234–35
Dean, Bentley 246–48
Denial Bay 14
desert oak 42
dingoes 8–10, 15, *30*, 104, 133–34, 136–37, 140–42, 148–49, 176–78, *177*, 199–200, 228–30, 237–38
Dixon, Len 17, 161–62, *163*
Dobbins, Bob and Leon 36–37
Dog Fence Act (SA) 7
Dog Fence Beach 4
Dog Fence Board (SA) 19, 39, 110

dogs (domestic) 44, 107
Dogwood Creek 236
Dulacca 236
Dunleavin 241
Durance, Dick 101

Edgley, Stephen 234
Edwards, Dave 206–7
Egerer, Carol and Wally 160
electrified fence 17, 20–21, 43
Emu Creek 116
Emu Well 117
emus 13, 56–58, 203, 208–10,
    220–23, *221*, 228–30
Euria Rockhole 29–31
Eyre, Edward John 4, 126,
    130, 139
Eyre Highway 18

Falconio, Peter 128, 212, 226
Fischer, Tim 2
Flannery, Tim 157
Flegg, Peter 175–88, *177*, *190*,
    204–8, 212, 231–32
Flinders, Matthew 5
Flinders Ranges 144, 146
Fossett, Steve 231
frog, trilling 122–24, *124*
Frome Downs Station 16, 151

Gahan, G. A. 128
Gee, Phil 114, 126
Giles, Ernest 49–52, 58–62,
    73
goannas 196
Grabovack, Ted 70–71
Graetz, Dean 145

Gray, Paul 194–97, *198*,
    200–1, 205, 209, 232
Great Australian Bight 1, 4–5
Great Victoria Desert 36
Greenfield, Keith 113–17
Greenfield, Lorraine 108, 114
Gregory Creek 126

Hamilton Gate Station 172,
    175
Hammat, Ricky 23–29, 246
Herbert, Jim 232–33
Holden, Phillip 187
Holland, Ian 50

Jackson, Stuart 86–87
Jaensch, Dean 71–72
Jimmy (Nanthona) 58–59, 61
Johnson, Michael 57

kangaroos 13, 120, 186,
    193–94
Kidd, Sandy 199–200
Kilmer, Val 77
King, Lindsay 120, 122
Koppio Smithy Museum
    36–37
kurrajong 230

Lake Eyre 126, 129–31
Lake Frome 144–46
Lake Torrens 125–26
Latz, Peter 27, 42, 47–48
Lawson, Henry 169
Leichhardt, Ludwig 236
Lester, Yami 67
Lewis, Max 233–34

Little, Frank 172
Lunney, Daniel 147

MacLachlan, Byron 7
MacLachlan, Hugh 70–71
McTaggart, Ian 7
Maher, Peter 186
Maralinga 65–68
Marree 128, 133
marsupial mice 121–22
marsupial moles 46
Martin, Colin, Shirley, Joyce
    and Suzanne 163–67
Mitchell, Bill 170
Mohr, Frances and Len
    172–76
Molden, Terry and Lorraine
    215
Moolawatana Station 134, 141
Morley Station 230
Morton, Peter 99–100, 106
Mount Eba Station 105
Mount Finke 48–49
Mount Hopeless 139
Mudla Creek 113
mulga 47
Muloorina Station 129–31
Mulpuddie, Charlie, Edie,
    Rosie and Henry 67
Mulyungarie Station 148
Munamerrie 198

Newsome, Alan 172
Nitschke, Rosslyn ('Toss') 105,
    107, 116
Nitschke, Slinger 105
Norwood, John 14–20, 56

Nuckulla Hill 44

Ocock Sandhills 4
Oldfield, Shane 132–35
O'Neil, Grant 171

Paisley, Peter 119–22
Paralana Hot Springs 150
Percival, Dinah 142,187
Pickard, John 170
Pieck, Anthony 121
pigs, feral 184
Pilkington, Doris 5
Price, Phoompy 28–29
prickly pear 241

quandong 27
Quinyambie Station 148, 157

rabbits 63, 119–21, 169–70
Rankin, Emma 95
Rankin, Sharon 85, 93–95,
    104
Rankin, Wayne 85–86, 93–95,
    97, 97–98, 102–5
Read, John 124, 148
Redford, Harry 200
Richards, Chris 23–26, 31
Roma 232–35
Roxby Downs 117–19
Ryreem Station 32

St Peter Island 35
Sandow, Bill 11–23, *21*,
    32–34, 38–48, 50–65,
    68–80, 82, 98, 125, 246
Schultz, Peter 205

scorpions 74, 171
Screech Owl Creek 126
Sheehan, Audrey 142–43
Sheehan, Gerard 142–43
Sheehan, Jane 143
Sheehan, Michael 134–35, 138, 140–43, *141*, 247
Shepard, Al 87
Shephard, Mark 67
'Skeeta' 210–11
Slim, Sir William 106–7
Smark, Peter 86
spinifex 32
Sprigg, Doug 143–47, 246–47
Stanley, Jerry 17, 179–85, 187–93, *190*, *195*, 207, 212–44
Stanley, Joyce 238
Stanley, Marie 226, 235
Stanley, Noel 227, 239
Stretton, Bill 105, *106*
Stuart, John McDouall 48, 115, 127
Stuart Creek 127
Sturt, Charles 44
Swift, Jonathan 34

Tambo 220
Tent Hill 116

Thijssen, Francis 34
thorny devils 46
Tilcha Station 164
traps 27–28, 37, *38*
Trewartha, Kym 33
Tuchyna, Thomas 125
Twins Station 92

Van Dyck, Steve 57

wagtails 136
Walker, Lucy 228
Watson, George Chale 169
Westney, Candida 142
White, Terry 194, 196, *198*, 200–1
Whitfield, Brett 213
Wilson, Alec 16, 150–54, *153*
Wilson, Deb 152–54
Witte, Ingrid 172
wombats 16, 20, 48, 236
Woodford, Angus 89
Woodford, Finn 91–92
Woomera 62, 96–102
Wynbring 54, 58–63, *60*, *62*

Yendall, Anthony 13–20
Yerilla Creek 139